POPSICLE-STICK-GRAFFITI

NUMBER THREE - BUBBLE LETTERS

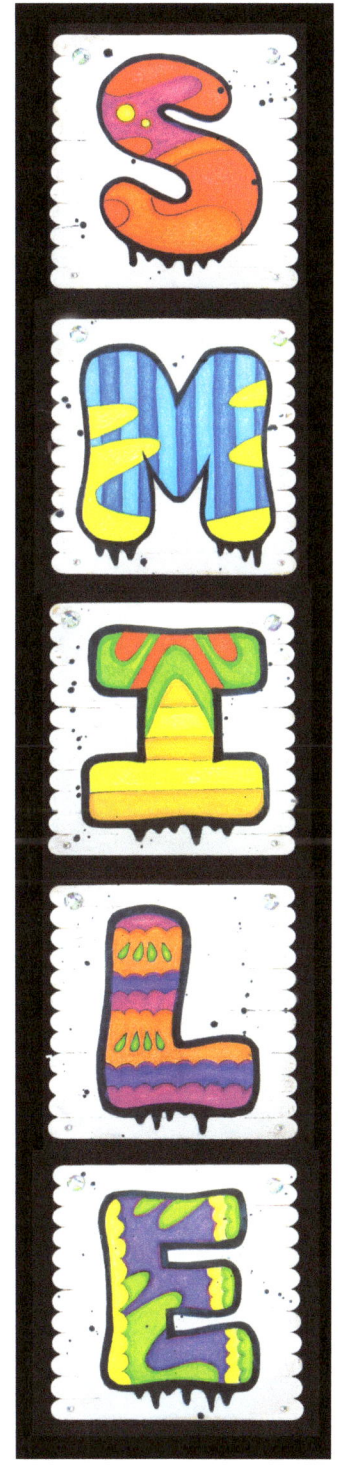

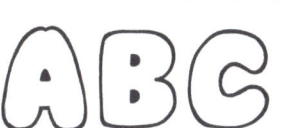

CONTENTS

INTRODUCTION
& SUPPLIES............... 3

PART ONE
TECHNIQUES....   4

PART TWO
PROJECTS

ABC............................ 18
BOO.......................... 22
PARTY....................... 26
SMILE....................... 32
THROWIES................. 36
FREESTYLE............... 37
SO FLY...................... 40
LIFE.......................... 44

PART THREE
LETTER
TEMPLATES............... 48

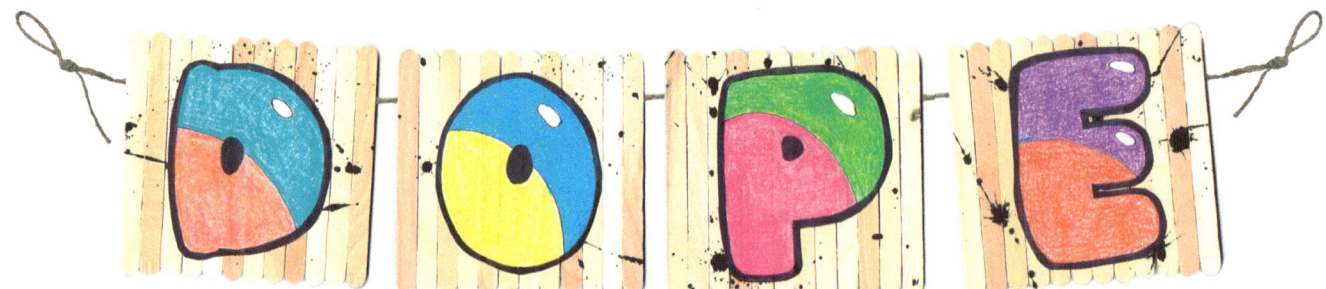

If you want to design your own bubble letters and other styles of graffiti, our two instructional books, 'Learn to Draw a Graffiti Master-Piece', and 'Why Write When You Can Tag: Learn To Draw The Best Graffiti Tags Ever' are a great place to learn graffiti lettering techniques.

OTHER BOOKS IN THIS SERIES:
Popsicle-Stick-Graffiti/ Number One/ Shapes
Popsicle-Stick-Graffiti/ Number Two/ Signs
Popsicle-Stick-Graffiti/ Number Four/ Mobiles

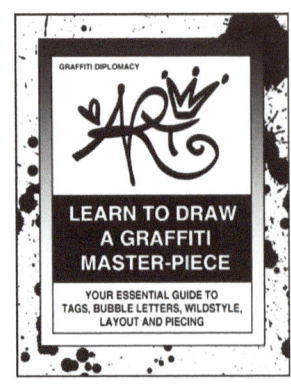

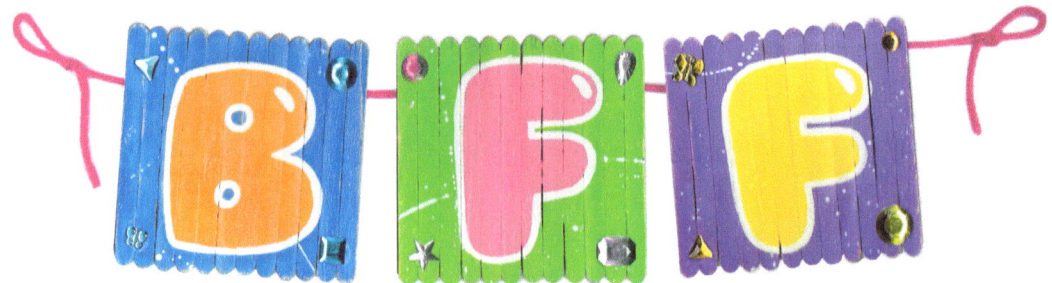

Popsicle-Stick-Graffiti /Number Three/ Bubble Letters
First Printing, 2018
ISBN-13: 978-0990438144
ISBN-10: 0990438147
Series: ® Popsicle-Stick-Graffiti
DISCLAIMER: Do not draw graffiti on any public or private surface without permission.
Find us on the web at "graffitidiplomacy.com"
For general information on our other products, please contact us at "graffitidiplomacy@yahoo.com"

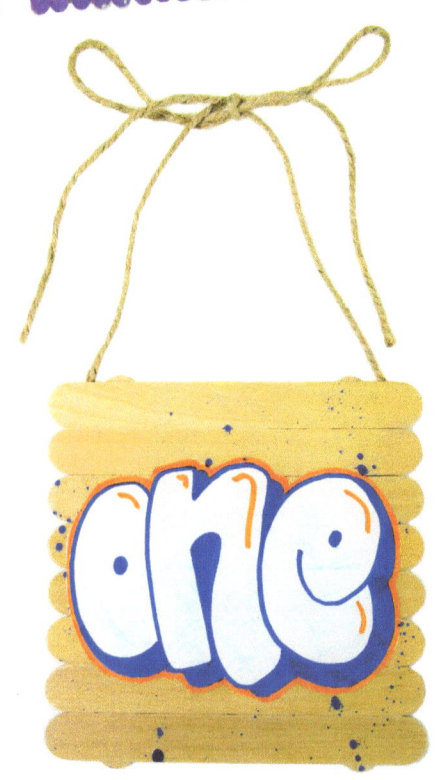

INTRODUCTION & SUPPLIES

Bubble letters are a popular style of graffiti lettering. This book will teach you to turn ordinary popsicle sticks and tongue depressors into stunning bubble letter art. All you have to do is copy the bubble letter templates from the back of the book, make them into paper stencils, and then trace the stencils onto paper or wood. You can color your bubble letters with acrylic paint, magic markers, crayons or colored pencils in exciting patterns and bright colors that vibrate with energy just like real graffiti. With just a few simple tools and the instructions in this book, there are no bounds to what you can create. You can apply finishing touches such as sequins, rhinestones, beads, or plastic ornaments from your local dollar store (like the plastic reptiles on the cover of this book) to transform your simple bubble letter projects into stunning artistic treasures that will last a lifetime.

Popsicle sticks are made from real wood so that means they are durable and water-resistant. They can be painted, sanded, and varnished just like real wood. All of the projects in this book are made with regular popsicle sticks or jumbo popsicle sticks (also known as tongue depressors). Regular popsicle sticks measure approximately 4 1/2" x 3/8". Jumbo popsicle sticks measure approximately 6" x 3/4". Exact sizes vary depending on the brand. Popsicle sticks sometimes have rough edges that can cause splinters so you need to take care when using them.

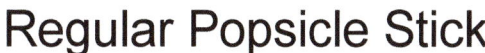

Regular Popsicle Stick

Jumbo Popsicle Stick

MATERIALS NEEDED
Regular Popsicle Sticks & Jumbo Popsicle Sticks
Tacky Glue (thicker and stronger than white glue)
Regular White Glue
String (yarn, hemp, rawhide, or any other kind)
Ribbon
Brown Kraft Paper - small pieces for hangers
Masking Tape & Clear Tape
Tracing Paper
#2 Pencil & Eraser
Acrylic Paints (tubes or jars)
Paintbrush/ Water Container/ Mixing Palette
Sharpie Fine-Point Permanent Marker - Black

Cheap Copy Paper - the kind you use in a printer
Magic Markers, Crayons, or Colored Pencils
Varnish or Shellac
Mod Podge (when using light-weight drawing paper)
Sandpaper - a variety of weights or grits
Clear Cellophane or Plastic Wrap
Good Quality Drawing Paper
Magnetic Tape
DECORATIVE ELEMENTS
Assorted Wood and Plastic Beads
Tree Branch or Wood Dowel
Rhinestones, Sequins, or Stickers
Plastic Ornaments from a Party Store or Dollar Store

IMPORTANT NOTES:
1) Sharpies are the magic marker of choice for graffiti artists. They are permanent so they dry instantly and won't smear. They are used primarily for outlining letters. When using Sharpies you must always put a piece of cardboard underneath the paper you are drawing on because Sharpies will leak through paper and stain your table.

2) Sandpaper is available in a variety of weights or grits. When using sandpaper always wear a dust mask and sand in a well-ventilated area, or go outside. Never breath in paint or wood dust.

3) If you decide to apply varnish, the magic markers you use must be permanent makers that are not water soluble. Test all of your tools out on scrap paper first. You can always skip the varnish if needed.

PART 1. TECHNIQUES

#1. BUILD THE PLAQUES

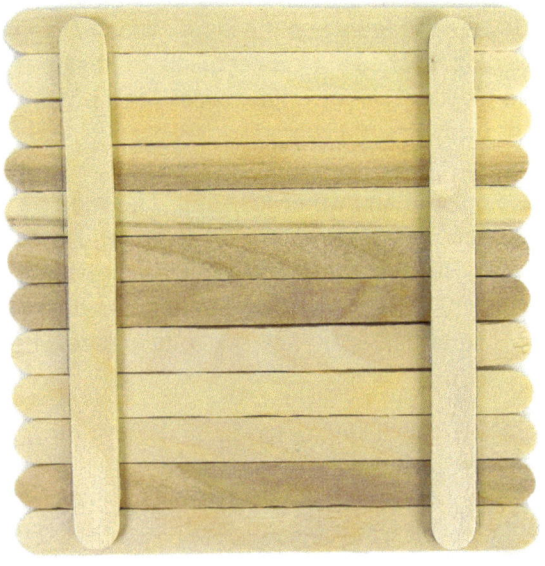

BACK VIEW

REGULAR POPSICLE STICK PLAQUE

Make sure all the sticks are flat and straight.
STEP 1. Lay down 12 sticks.
STEP 2. Glue on two sticks across to hold the plaque together.

You can rotate the plaque and hang this way, too.

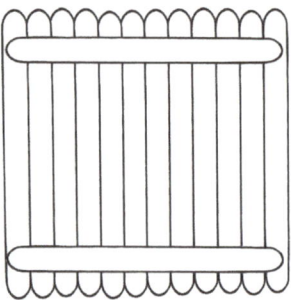

Use thick tacky glue whenever possible to hold the popsicle sticks together. You can buy it at your local craft store or art shop. When the glue is dry, rub both sides of your plaque with a cool damp cloth. This will help seal the wood and make it easier to paint on, plus prevent too much warping. Let the plaque dry thoroughly.

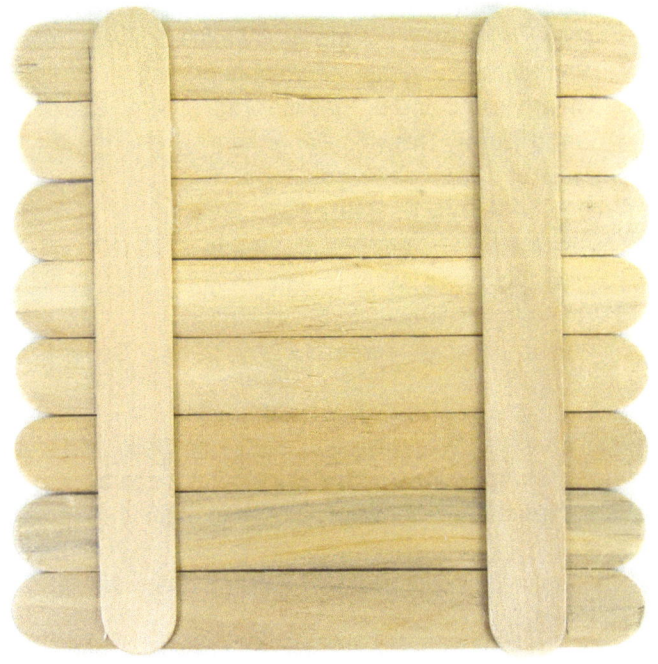

BACK VIEW

JUMBO POPSICLE STICK PLAQUE

Make sure all the sticks are flat and straight.
STEP 1. Lay down 8 sticks.
STEP 2. Glue on two sticks across to hold the plaque together.
You can double the two crossed sticks for extra strength. That's up to you. Experiment and see what works best.

You can rotate the plaque and hang it this way, too.

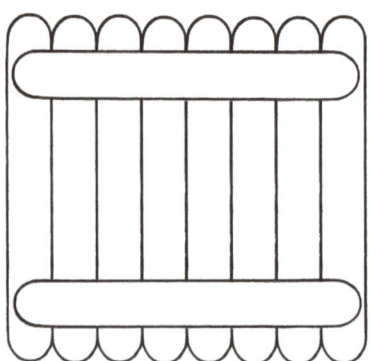

#2. MAKE AND ATTACH HANGERS

This technique works the same way with either regular or jumbo popsicle sticks.

STEP 1. Cut two small rectangular tabs from brown kraft paper or a grocery store bag.
STEP 2. Glue the tabs onto a stick over the ends of a piece of string or ribbon, like little band-aids.
STEP 3. Turn over and glue the stick to the back of a plaque.

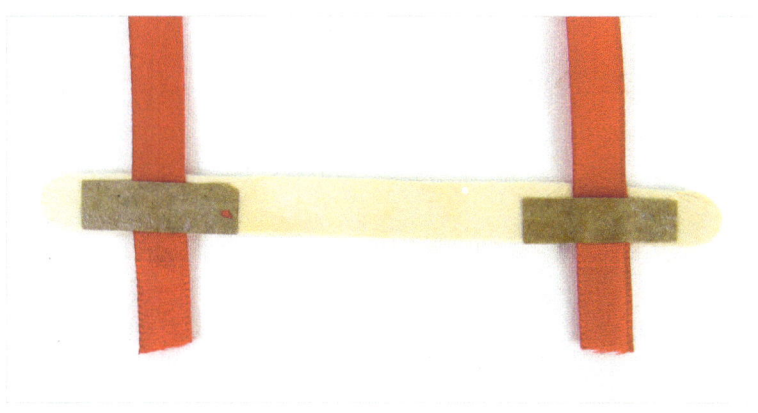

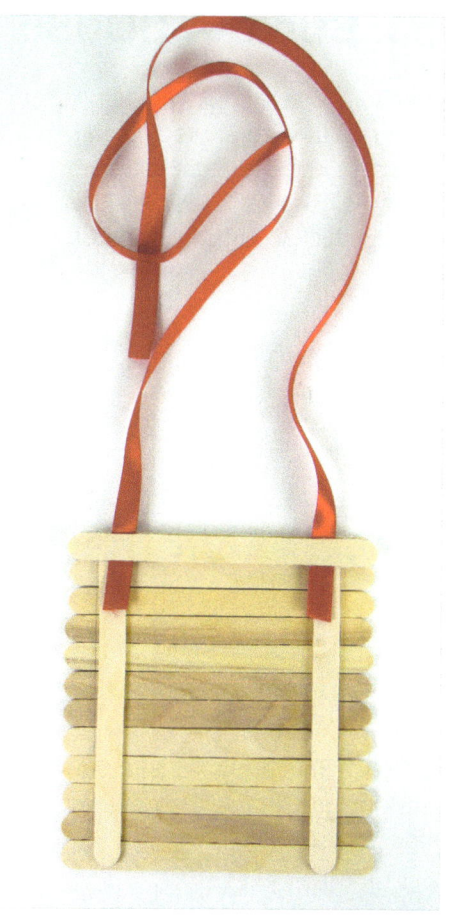

BACK VIEW

You can use any kind of string you like but my favorite is twine or hemp. It coordinates well with the natural look of wood sticks.

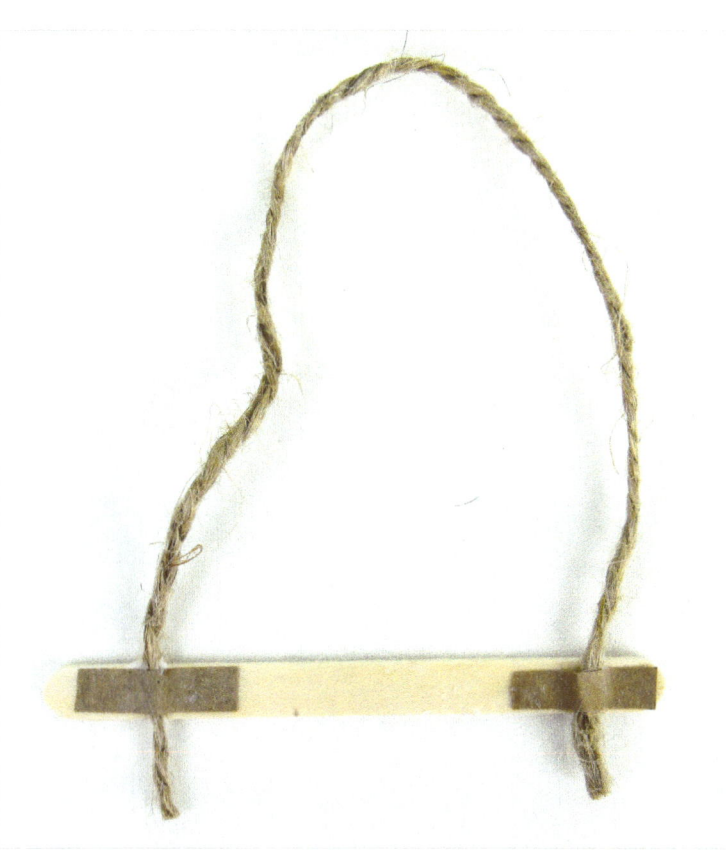

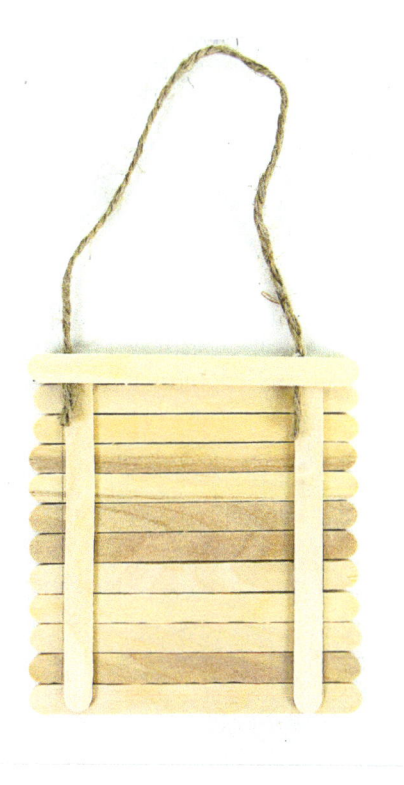

BACK VIEW

#3. BUILD A HOUSE

Jumbo popsicle sticks are thinner than regular size sticks and can be easily cut with a pair of sharp scissors. Regular popsicle sticks are too thick to cut with scissors.

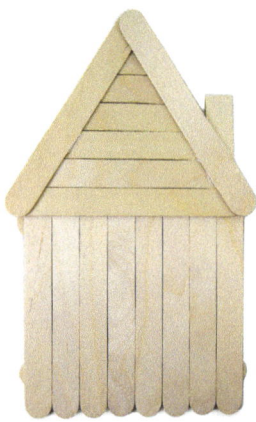

STEP 1. To start, build a jumbo stick plaque for the body of the house (see page 4).

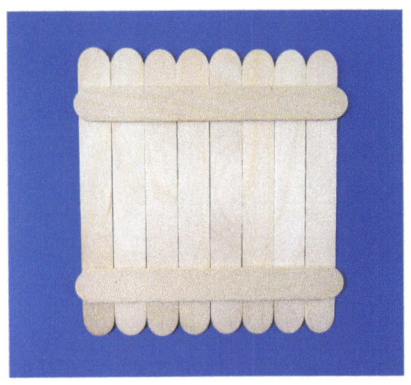

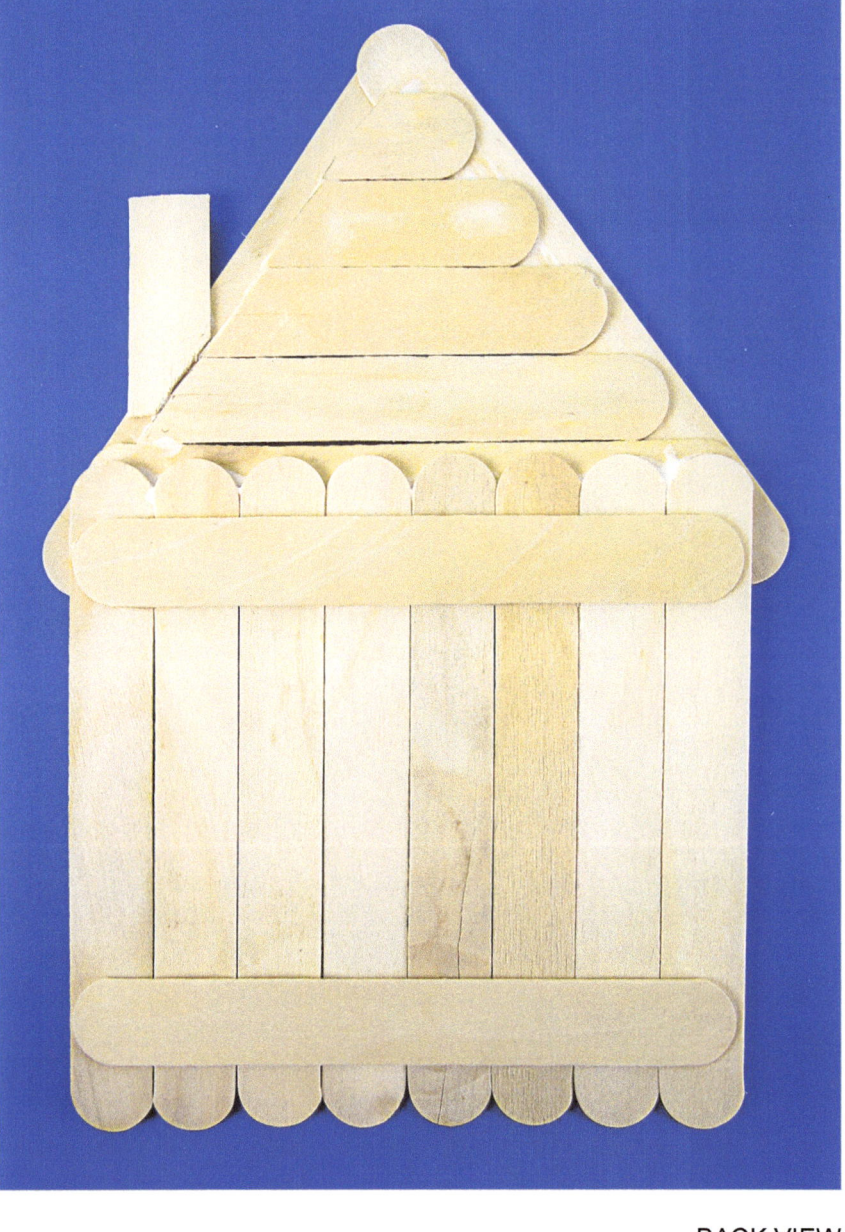

BACK VIEW

STEP 2. To build the roof, form a triangle with three jumbo sticks and glue the ends together.

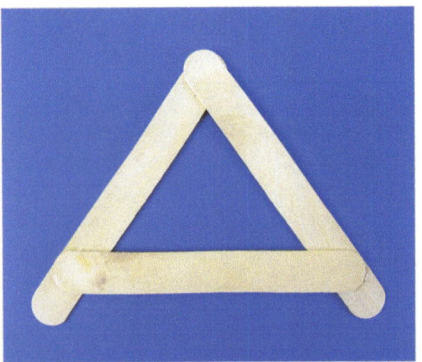

STEP 3. Cut jumbo sticks on an angle to fit inside the triangle. Glue them in place.

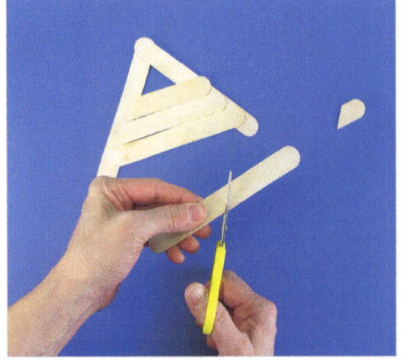

STEP 4. Fill in the whole triangle to complete the roof.

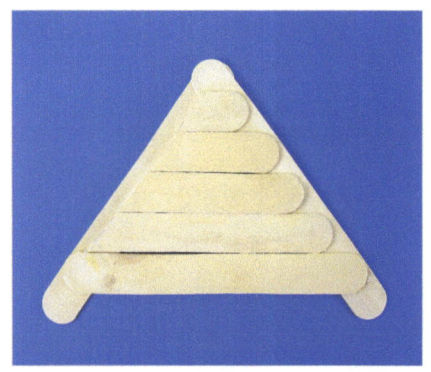

STEP 5. Make a chimney. Glue onto the roof.

STEP 6. Glue the roof onto the house.

HANGER ON BACK: Cut a piece of brown kraft paper in a triangle shape to fit on the top of the roof. Cut a small piece of string and form a loop. Glue the loop underneath the piece of kraft paper. Leave a little space between the two ends of the string.

Use any type of string to hang the house. I prefer natural twine, but colored string looks great, too.

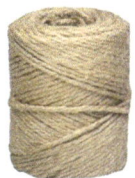

TWINE

ALTERNATE: Glue a sawtooth picture hanger to the back of the house with thick tacky glue. Give the glue plenty of time to dry before hanging on a wall.

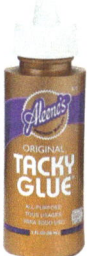

Tacky glue is my glue of choice for these projects because it is thicker and stronger than regular white glue.

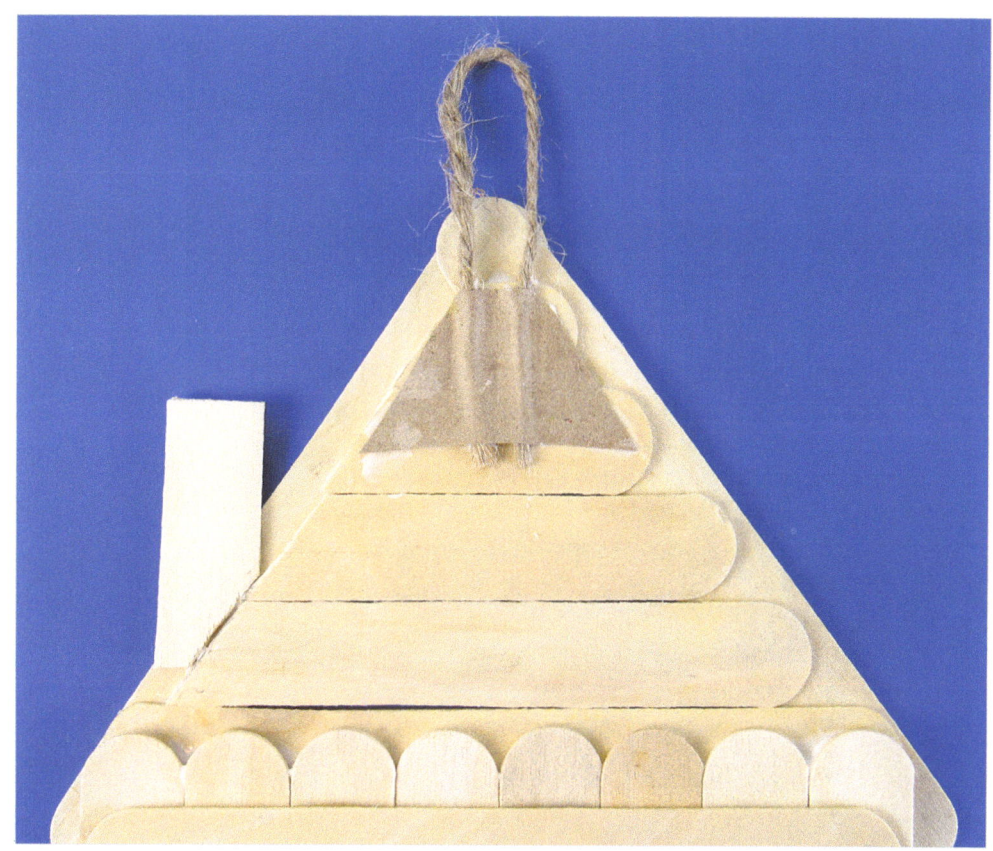

BACK VIEW

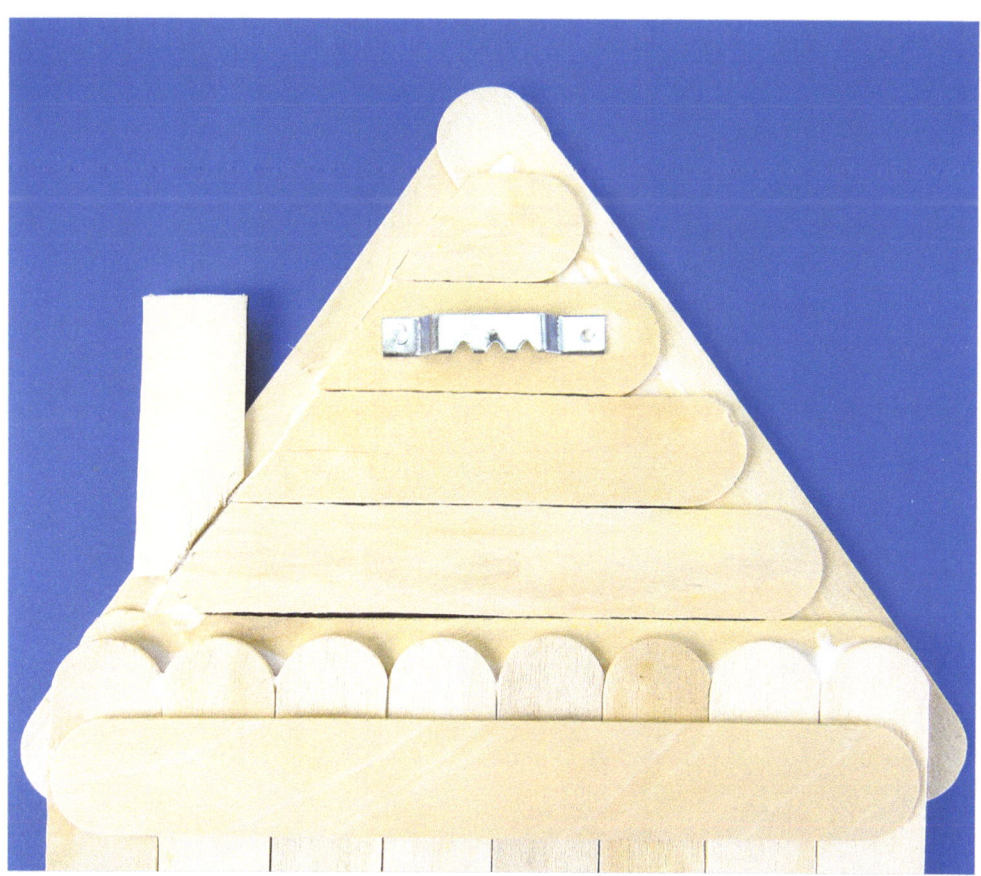

BACK VIEW

#4. STRING PLAQUES TOGETHER

USE THESE INSTRUCTIONS TO STRING TOGETHER REGULAR POPSICLE STICKS OR JUMBO STICKS

VERTICAL ARRANGEMENT

STEP 1. Measure two pieces of string long enough to hang the whole wall hanging. Tie a knot at the top.
STEP 2. Starting at the top plaque, apply glue to the inside edge of a crossed stick on one side.
STEP 3. Press the string into the glue, against the edge of the stick.
STEP 4. Glue on a second stick next to the first, with the string sandwiched tightly in between.
STEP 5. Repeat on the other side.
STEP 6. Attach all the plaques.

3
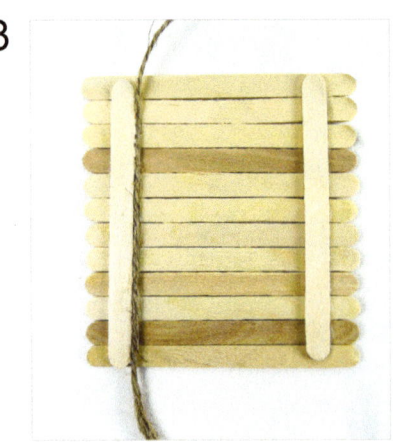

4
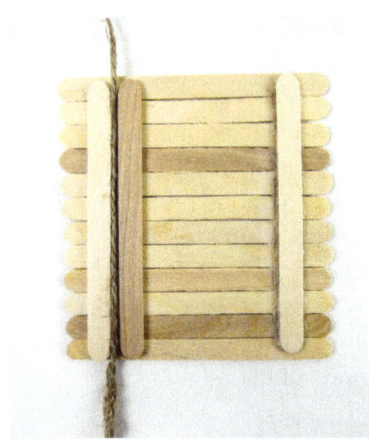

6a
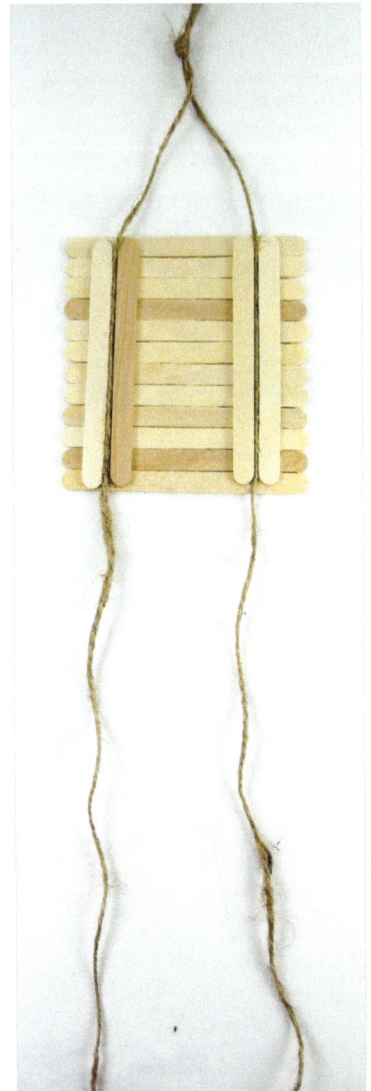

6b
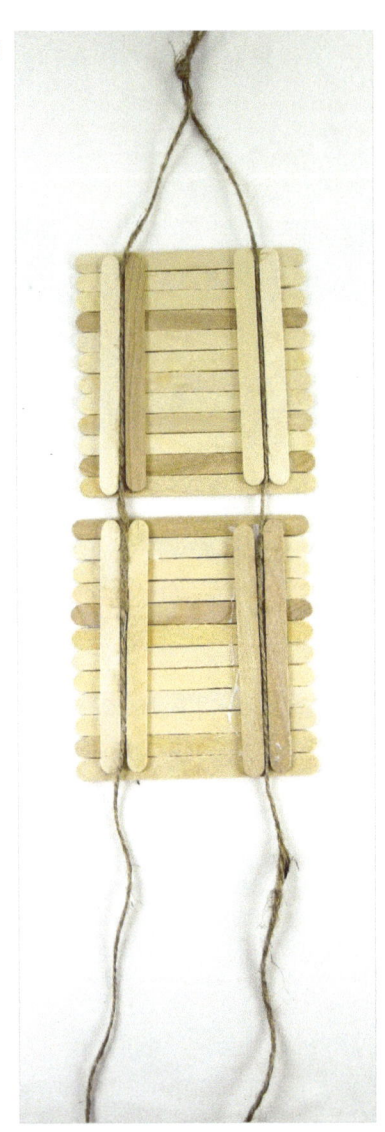

6c
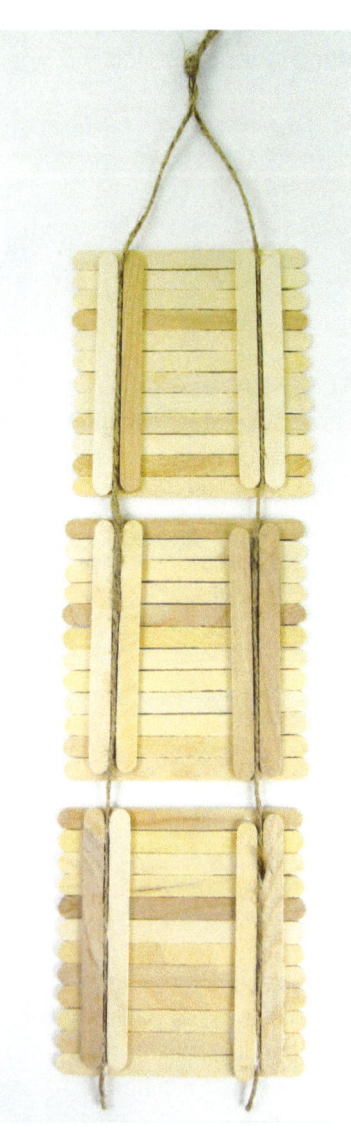

HORIZONTAL ARRANGEMENT

STEP 1. Measure a piece of string long enough for the whole wall hanging.
STEP 2. Starting with the middle plaque, apply glue in the crevice underneath the top stick.
STEP 3. Find the center of the string and press it into the glue in the crevice.
STEP 4. Glue another stick directly underneath, sandwiching the string in between the two sticks.
STEP 5. Attach the rest of the plaques, one at a time, on each side of the middle plaque.

4

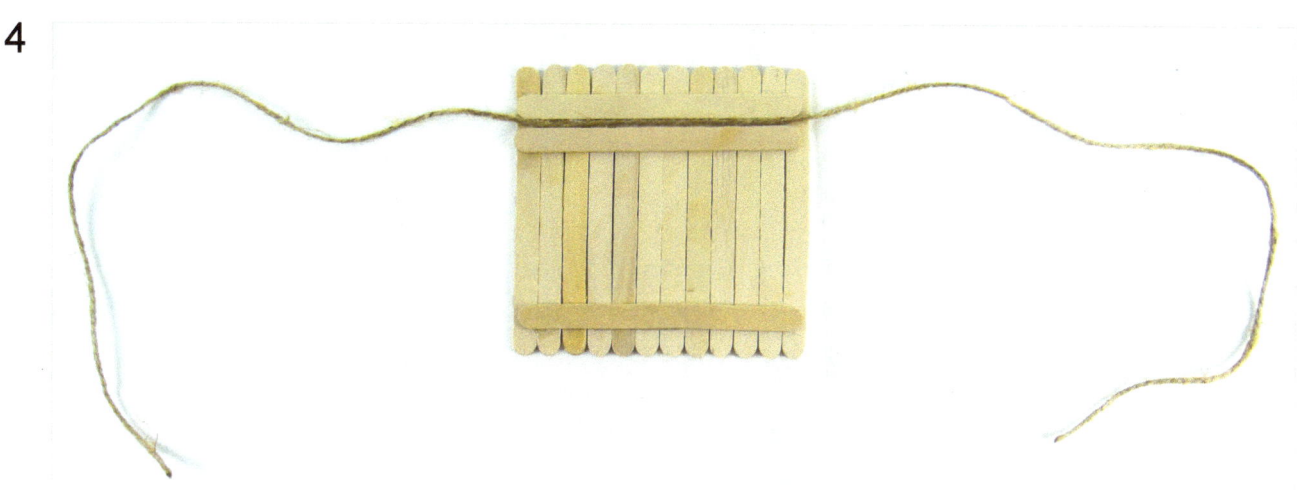

5

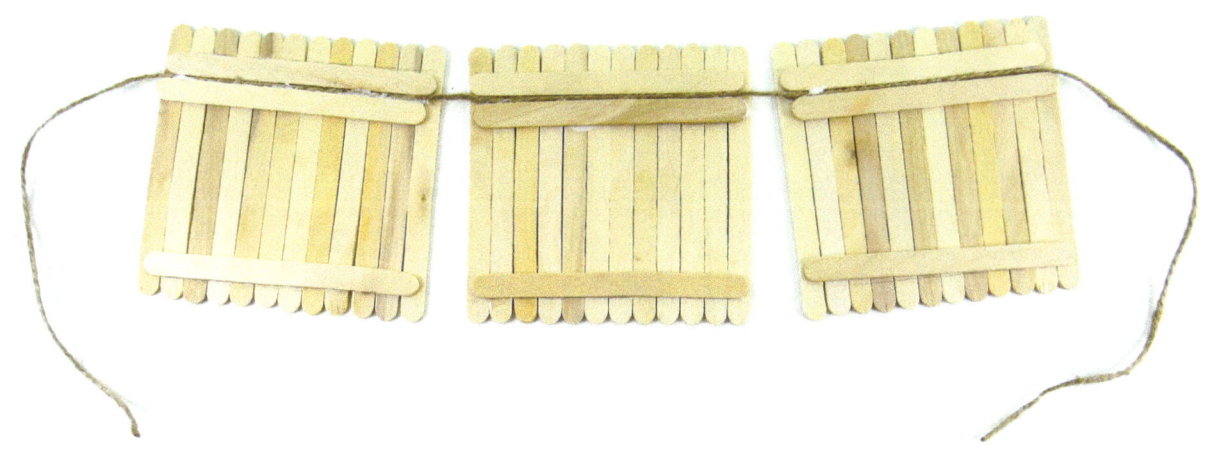

#5. MAGNETIC TAPE

Instead of using ribbon or string why not attach a few strips of self-stick magnetic tape to your popsicle stick plaque. Then stick it onto your refrigerator or your locker. You can buy rolls of magnetic tape at an office supply store or craft store. You can also buy magnetic sheets with adhesive on the back that you can cut to any shape.

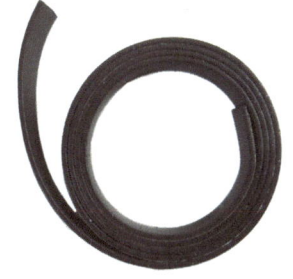

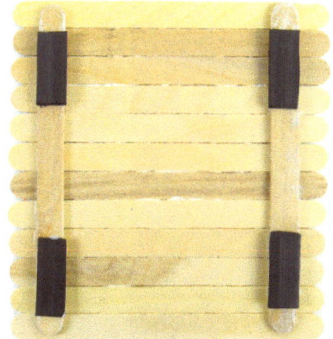

#6. MAKE THE STENCILS

OVERVIEW: The stencils you will need to complete the projects in this book are made by tracing the letter templates from pages 48-57 onto thin copy paper or tracing paper. Once you have the letters traced, cover the tracings with tape front and back. Cut them out. These are your reusable bubble letter stencils. The tape makes the stencils sturdy and water resistant. Trace the stencils onto wood plaques or drawing paper. Color the letters with your choice of markers, pencils, paint, or crayons.

A Sharpie Fine Point Permanent Marker is the perfect tool for outlining your bubble letters.

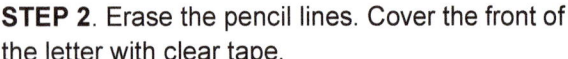

STEP 1. To begin, place a piece of thin copy paper or tracing paper on top of a page in this book (pages 48-57) and trace a letter with a pencil. Remove your paper from the book and draw over the pencil lines with a black Sharpie or any other dark marking tool.

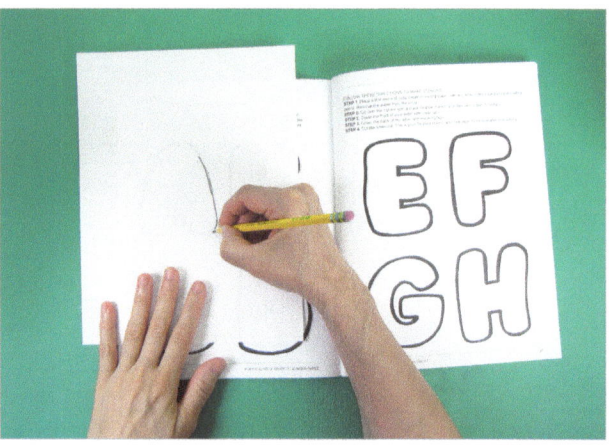

STEP 2. Erase the pencil lines. Cover the front of the letter with clear tape.

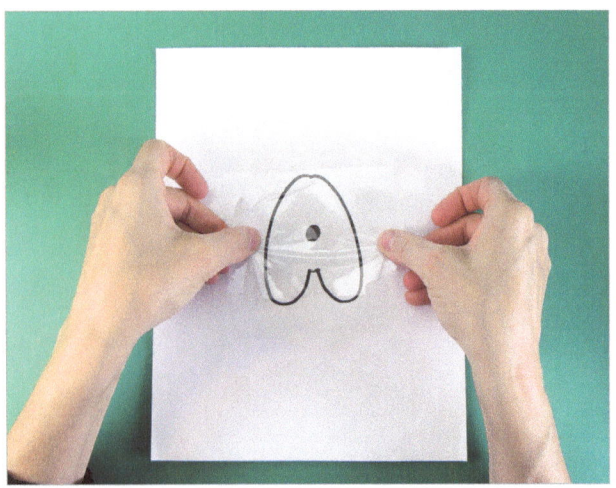

STEP 3. Turn your paper over and cover the back of the letter with masking tape.

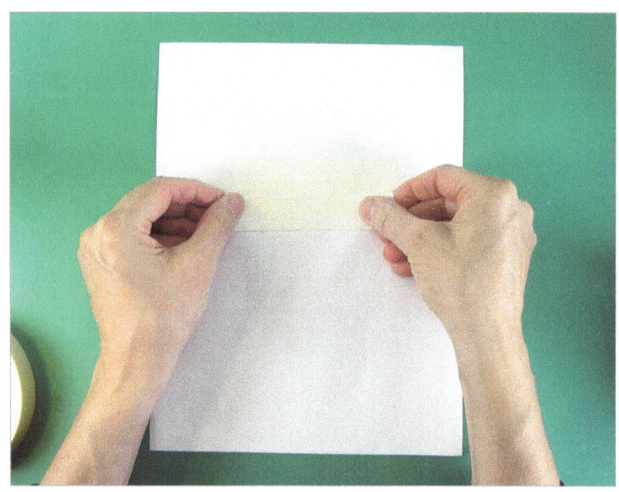

STEP 4. Cut the letter out including the black outline.

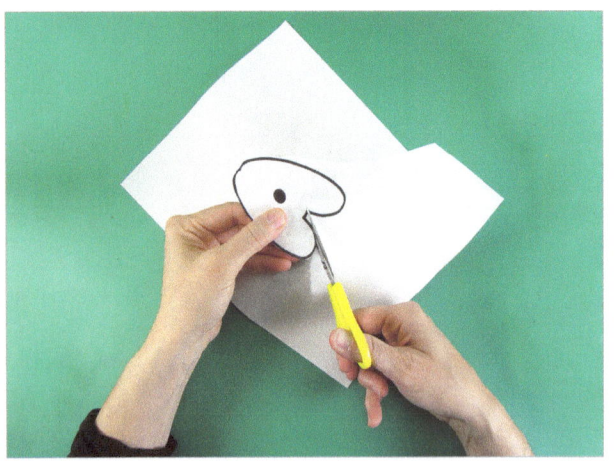

STEP 5. This is your finished stencil. The tape covering makes it sturdy and reusable dozens of times.

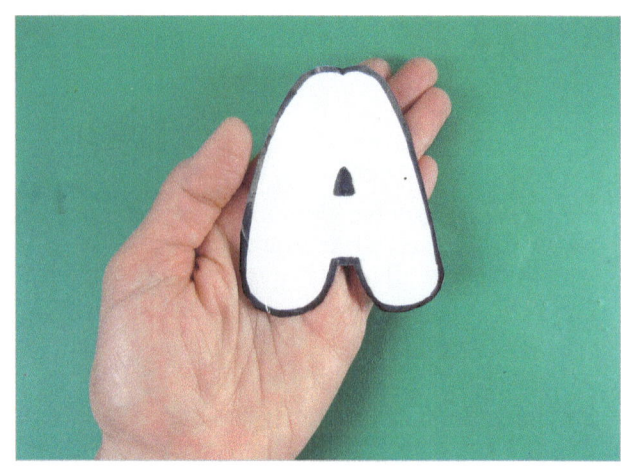

STEP 6. Place the stencil onto a regular size wood plaque. Hold it firmly in place with your fingertips and trace around the outside edge with a pencil.

STEP 7. If you need a guide to indicate where the hole should be placed, fold the stencil in half and position it back over the outline. Mark the hole.

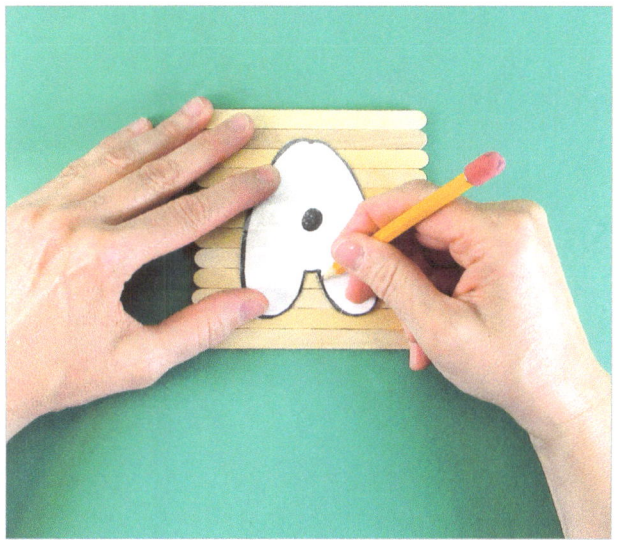

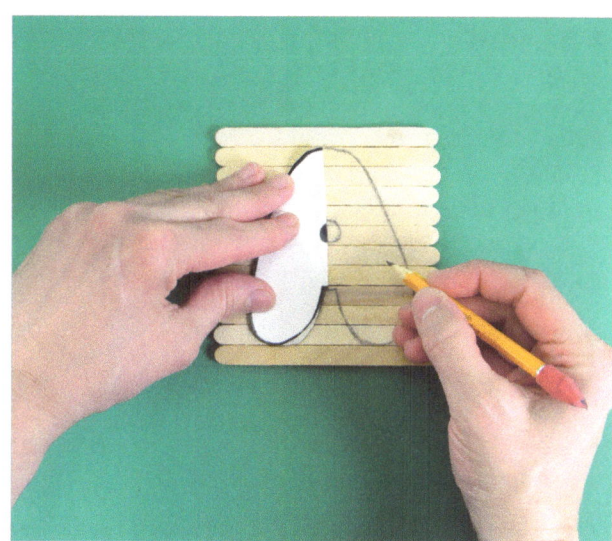

#7. PAINT THE LETTERS

STEP 1. Paint the letter anyway you like.

STEP 2. Paint the background.

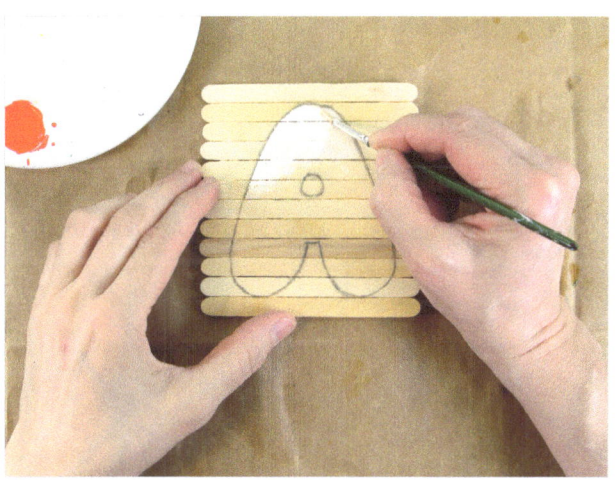

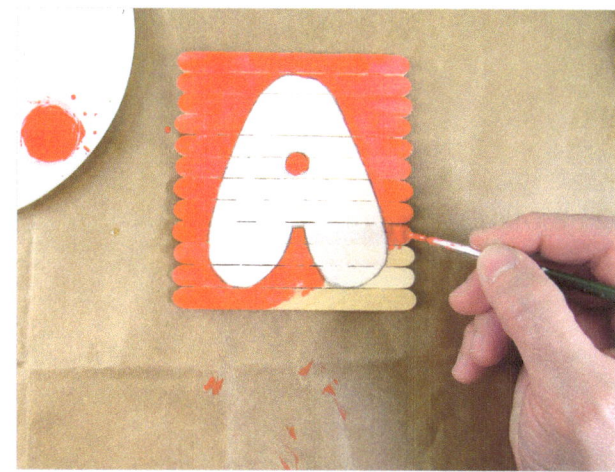

STEP 3. The first coat of paint you apply will be absorbed into the wood surface because wood is porous. So you will need to apply several coats to build up the color and make it vibrant.

STEP 4. When you are happy with your work, you can splatter paint onto your design using one of the techniques described on page 17.

STEP 5. Apply a coat of varnish for a water-resistent, professional finish.

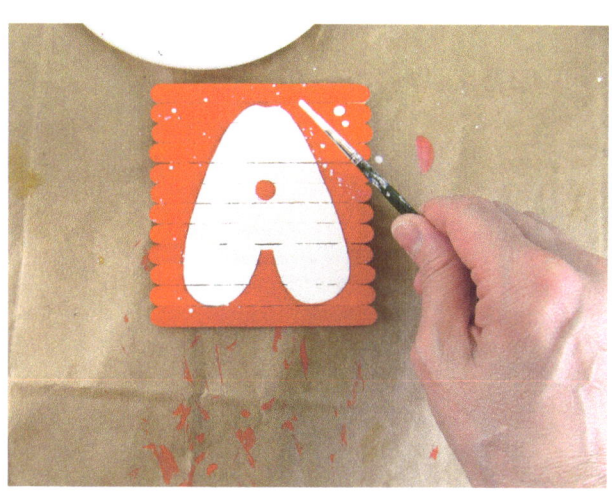

#8. MAKE PAPER CUTOUTS

Bubble letter paper cutouts are easy to make and are less messy then painted letters. All you really need are a box of crayons and regular white glue. You will also need a sheet of good quality drawing paper on which to trace your bubble letter stencils. A coat of Mod Podge applied to the back of the paper letter will make it sturdier and easier to handle. But Mod Podge is optional, and only necessary if the drawing paper is light-weight. You can paint your wood plaque or just leave it natural. Add small details like splashes and paint drips with a small brush and acrylic paint.

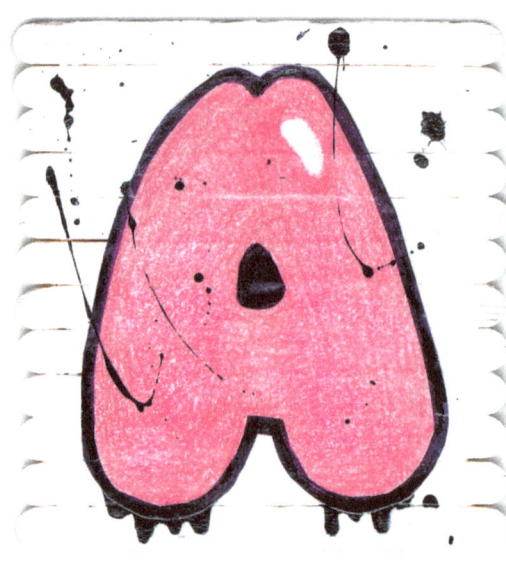

Mod Podge can be purchased at a craft store. When using Mod Podge, clean your brushes with soap and water after each use to prevent hardening.

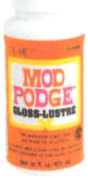 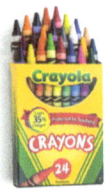

STEP 1. With a pencil, trace a bubble letter stencil onto a piece of good quality drawing paper.

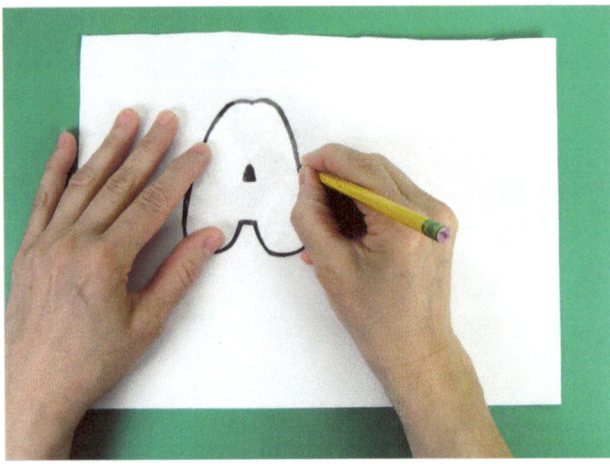

STEP 3. Color the bubble letter with a crayon, colored pencil, or magic marker.

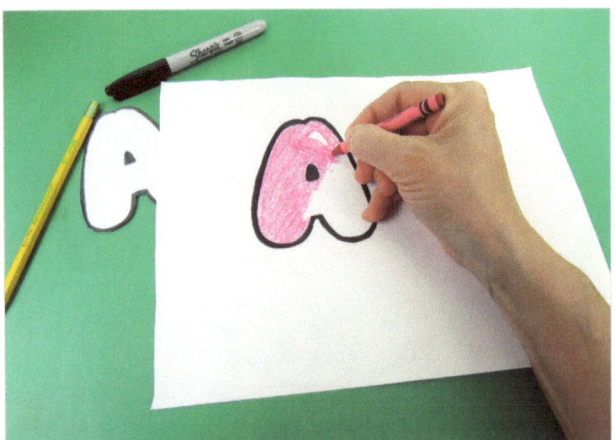

STEP 2. Go over the outline with a dark marker. Erase the pencil lines.

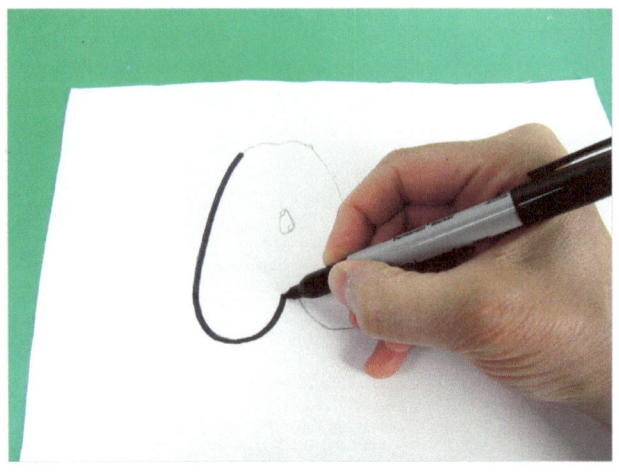

STEP 4. OPTIONAL: If the paper is light-weight, turn it over and apply a coat of Mod Podge to the back.

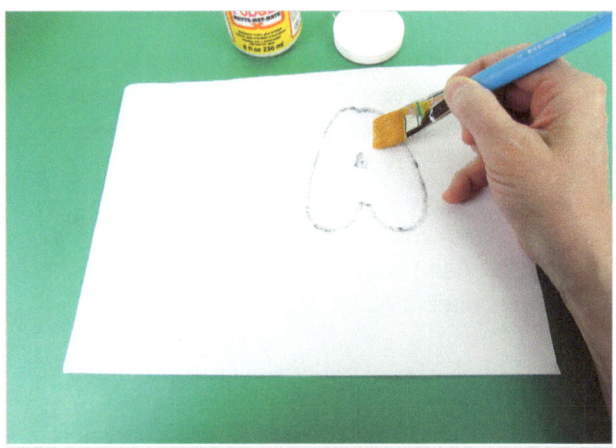

STEP 5. When the paper is dry, cut out the letter making sure to include the outline.

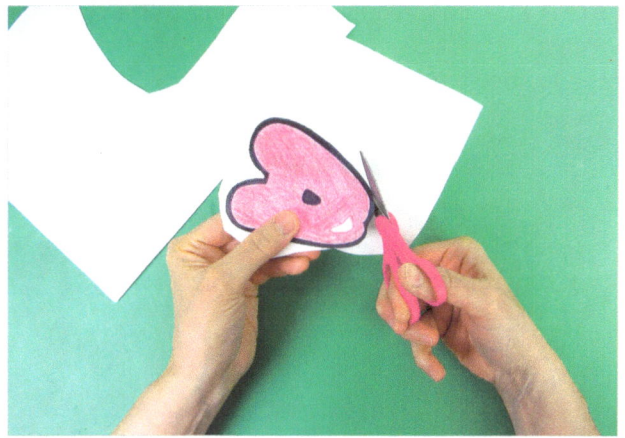

STEP 6. Apply white glue to the back. Spread it evenly around with a glue brush or with your finger.

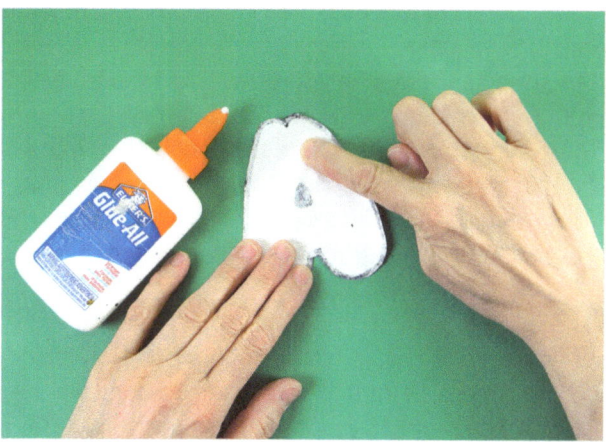

STEP 7. Position the letter where you want it to go and press down onto the plaque. Put a piece of clear plastic cellophane or wrap over the letter and smooth out any glue bubbles. Remove the plastic.

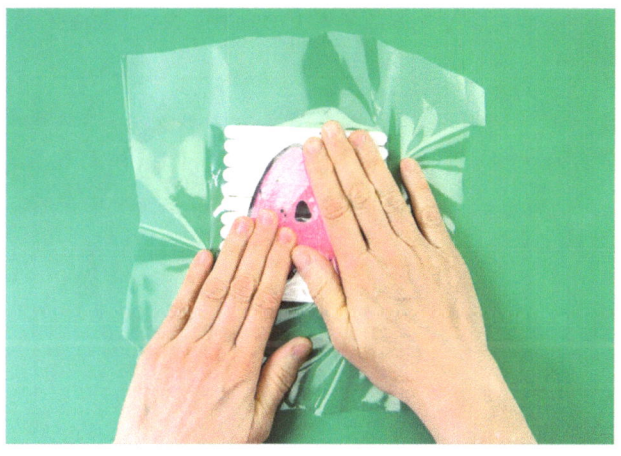

STEP 8. Mix up some paint with a little water in a small container. Splash with a paint brush. You may want to do your splashing <u>before</u> you glue the letter onto the plaque to prevent mistakes. Your choice.

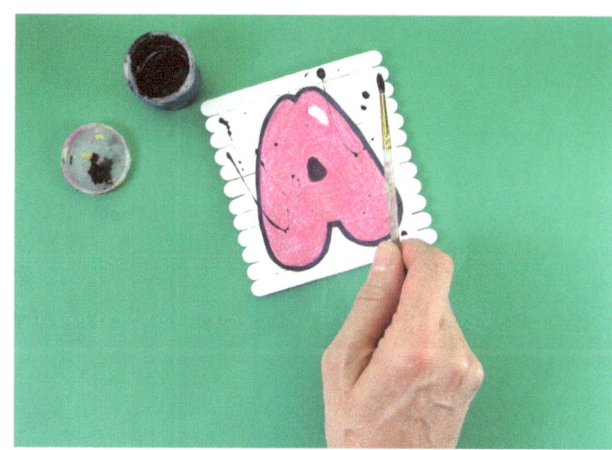

STEP 9. OPTIONAL: Draw little drips along the bottom edge of the letter with a pencil, and then paint them in with a small brush. Let the paint dry.

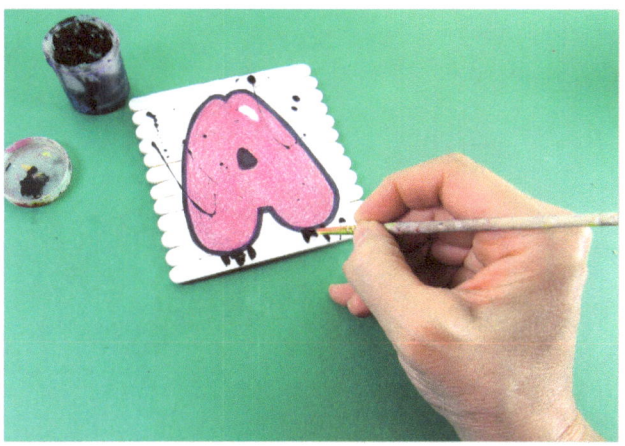

STEP 10. To finish, apply a coat of water-based varnish to each section of the design separately so the colors don't bleed into each other. When dry, apply a second coat across the whole piece.

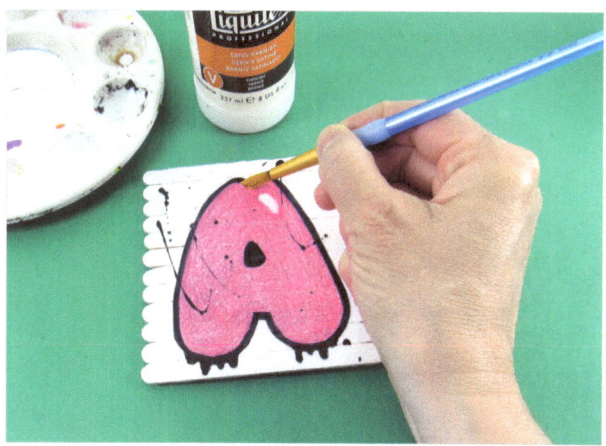

#9. DESIGN YOUR OWN BUBBLE LETTERS FROM SCRATCH

Each project in this book has bubble letter templates included to make it super-easy for you to complete the projects. But you may decide you'd like to try your hand at designing your own bubble letters. Plus, the bubble letter templates found on pages 48-54 (not counting the B and O for BOO) are sized to fit on regular size plaques, not on jumbo plaques. So you will need to enlarge those letters yourself.

The following technique will come in handy whenever you need to create bubble letters from scratch or modify smaller letters to make them larger. Use the diagram on page 15 (opposite page) as a guide to sketch out and design your own bubble letters in any size you need. Make them fat and bubbly.

STEP 1. Trace a regular size or jumbo size plaque onto a piece of copy paper. You only need to use cheap copy paper for this technique.

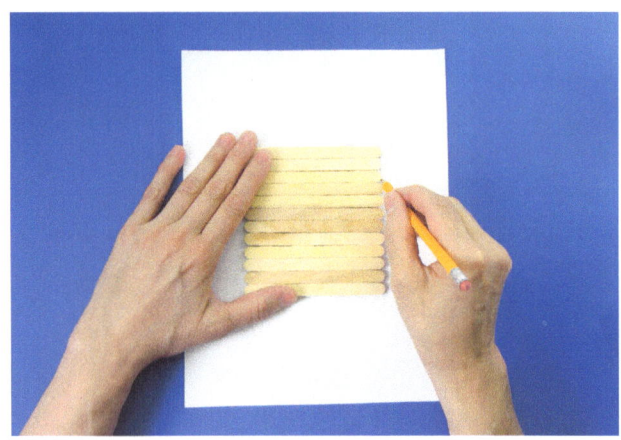

STEP 2. With a pencil, sketch ovals inside the plaque tracing to form the letter (see page 15).

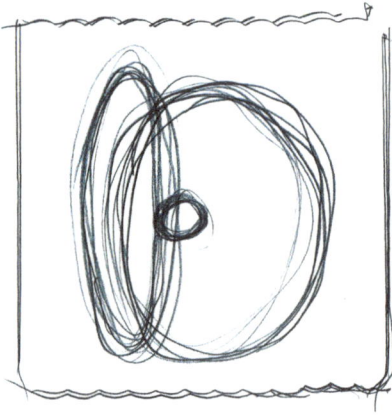

STEP 3. Draw around the outline with a dark marker.

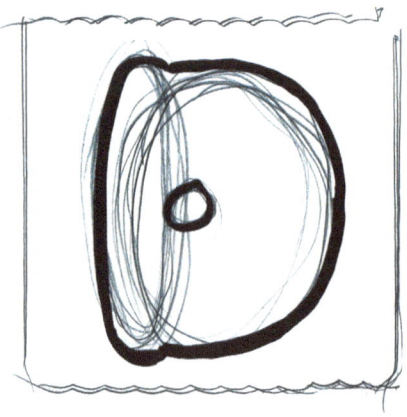

STEP 4. Erase the pencil lines.

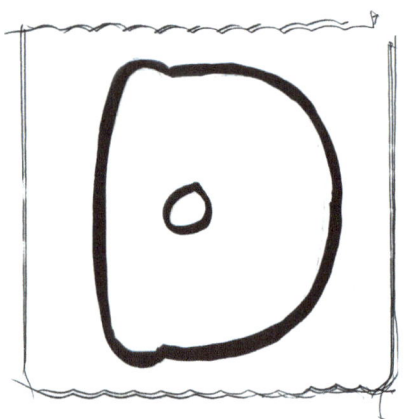

STEP 5. To make the drawing into a stencil, cover with tape and cut the letter out (see instructions on page 10).

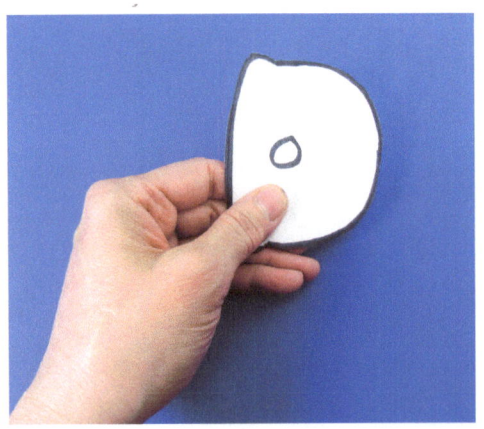

STEP 6. Trace the stencil onto a piece of good drawing paper. Color the bubble letter however you like and make a cutout (pages 12-13). Or just trace stencil directly onto wood and paint (page 11).

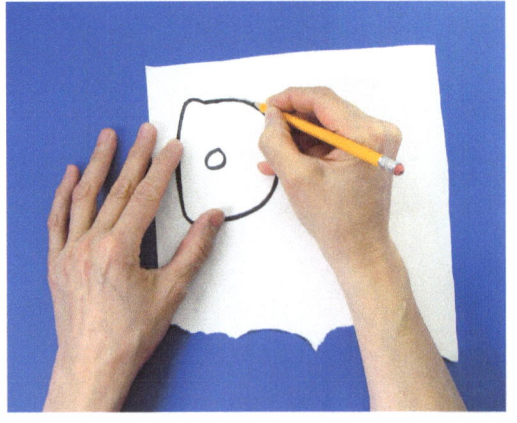

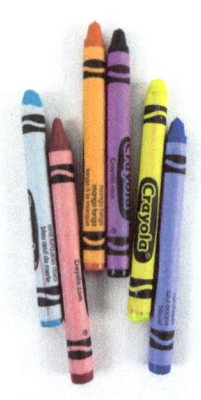

You can make stencils for this DOPE wall hanging using the diagram below. Make cutouts (see pages 12-13), outline with a black Sharpie, and color with crayons. I left the wood plaques natural and just splattered them with a bit of black paint, then varnished them. NOTE: You have the option to use the stencils made from the templates on pages 48-54. I just wanted to include a method you can use to design your own bubble letters from scratch.

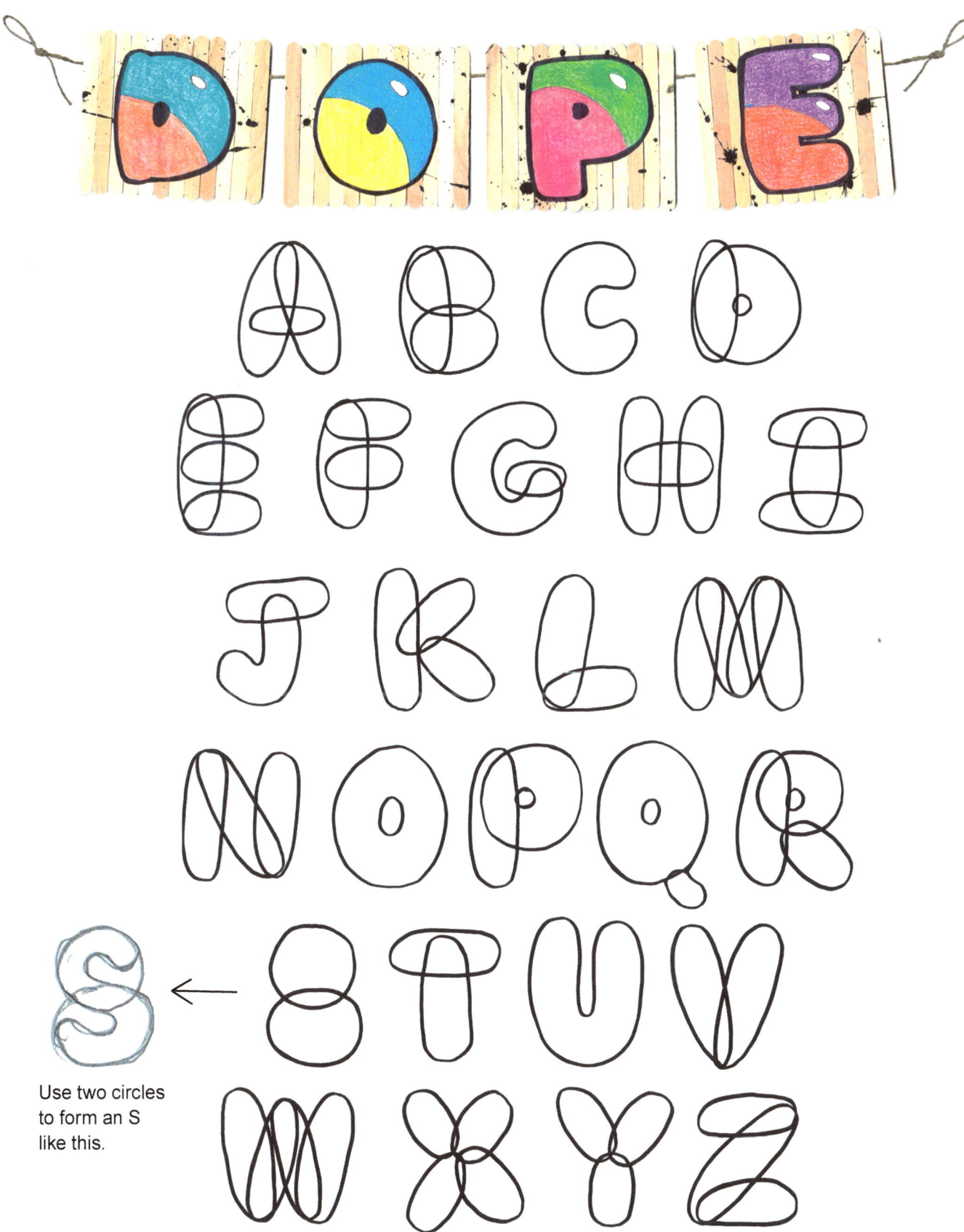

Use two circles
to form an S
like this.

#10. PAINTING TECHNIQUES

There are many different kinds of finishes you can use to decorate your wall hangings. Popsicle sticks contain all the natural beauty of real wood so you can use the same finishing techniques a furniture maker might use. Or you can apply a thick coat of acrylic paint like a painter. There are lots of possibilities. My personal favorite is to paint them with a few thin coats of acrylic paint, then use sandpaper to give my wall hangings a rustic, worn-out look. This is called *distressing*.

IMPORTANT: If you use sandpaper to *distress* your wall hangings, you must wear a **dust mask** and sand your project in a **well-ventilated area**. Or go outside.

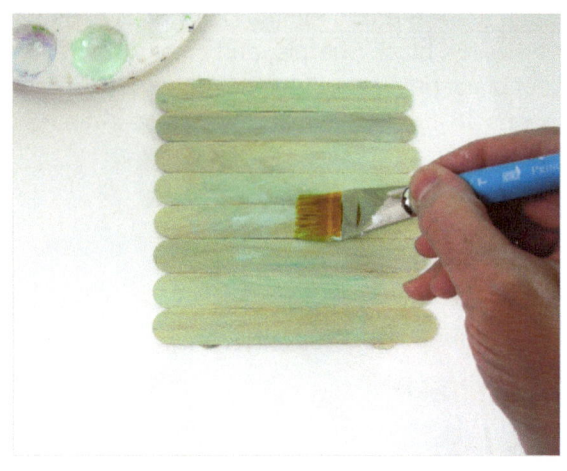

TO CREATE A DISTRESSED LOOK:
STEP 1. Paint the entire piece with a coat of watery paint. Let it dry.

STEP 2. Paint on several coats, building up the color. Apply a final coat of paint that has less water mixed in. Let the wood dry.

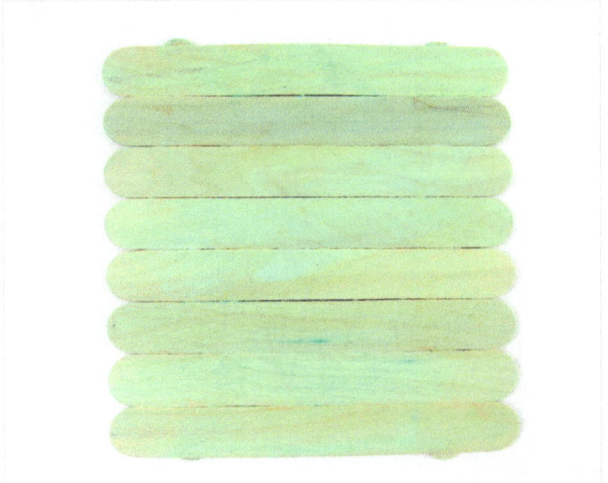

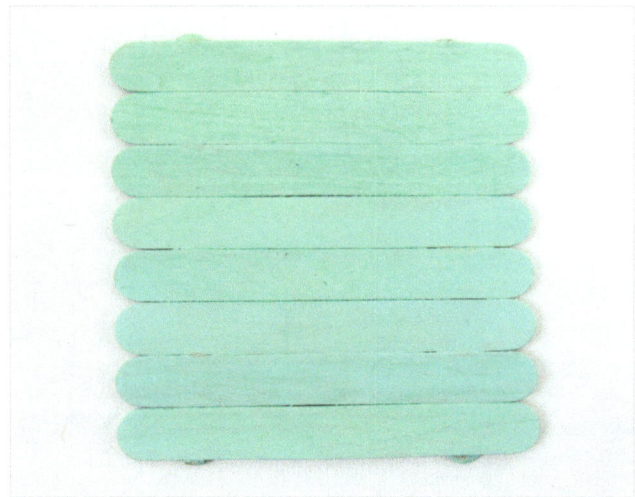

STEP 3. Once the paint is dry, rub a piece of sandpaper over the surface to distress the sticks. Rub harder on the edges, then gently across the middle.

STEP 4. Optional: Mix a <u>minuscule</u> bit of brown paint with some water. Brush onto the spots where the paint is sanded off and the wood is showing through.

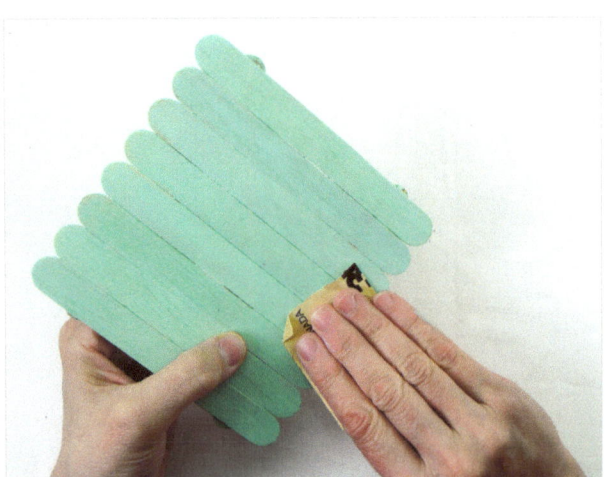

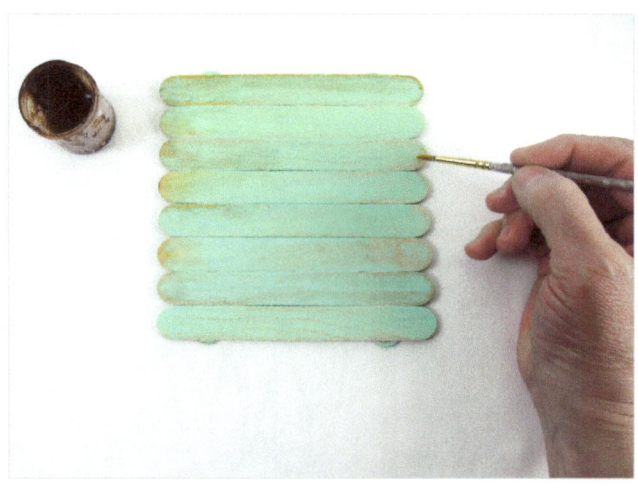

Let the piece dry thoroughly. The brown paint makes the finished plaque look old and worn. You can stop here and rub the piece lightly with sandpaper. Use fine-grit sandpaper for a slightly distressed look or large-grit sandpaper to remove more paint.

OPTIONAL: You can add another coat of paint in a different color, allowing some of the color from the bottom layers to show through. When dry, splatter the surface with a contrasting paint color of your choice, using any of the methods described below.

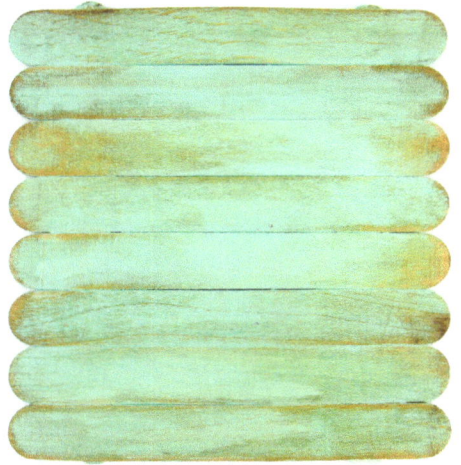

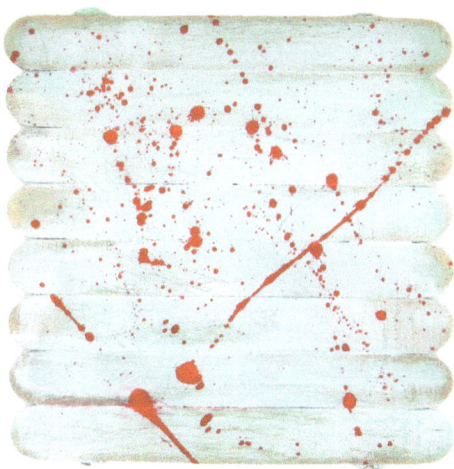

#11. PAINT SPLATTERING

Toothbrush Splatter - Dip the bristles of an old toothbrush in paint and run your finger over the top. Aim the toothbrush tip in the direction you want the dots to fall. The paint dots will be tiny.

Paintbrush Splatter - Dip a paintbrush in some paint and shake it over the surface of your plaque. The results will be drops that are bigger than a toothbrush. Swing your hand hard to create trails and streaks.

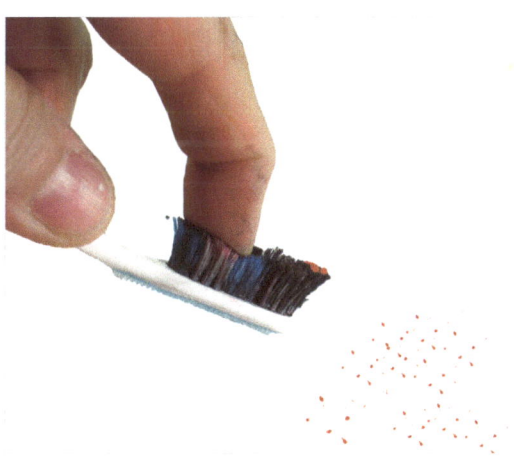

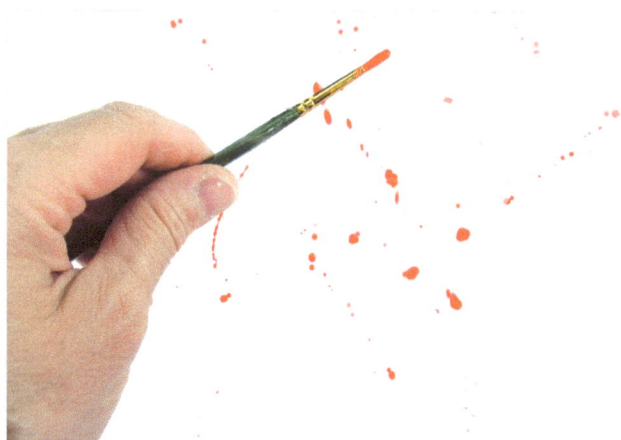

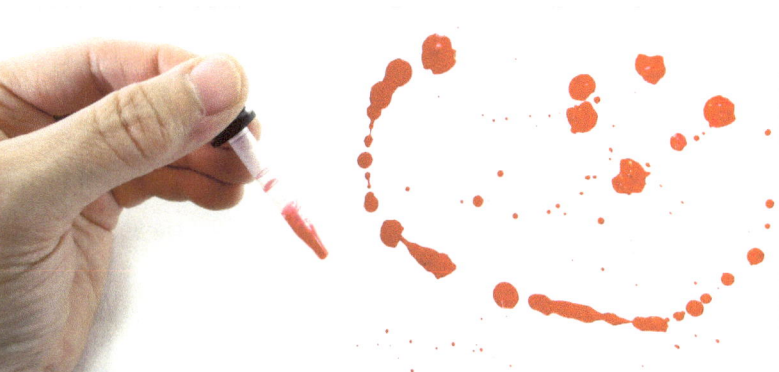

Eyedropper Splatter - Mix up some paint with water. Fill an eyedropper with paint and squeeze out a few drops onto your project. These drops will be really big, so practice on paper first.

Make splatter patterns before or after you apply letters to your plaque. NOTE: Paint splattering can get messy so cover your work area and wear an apron to protect your desk and clothes.

ABC

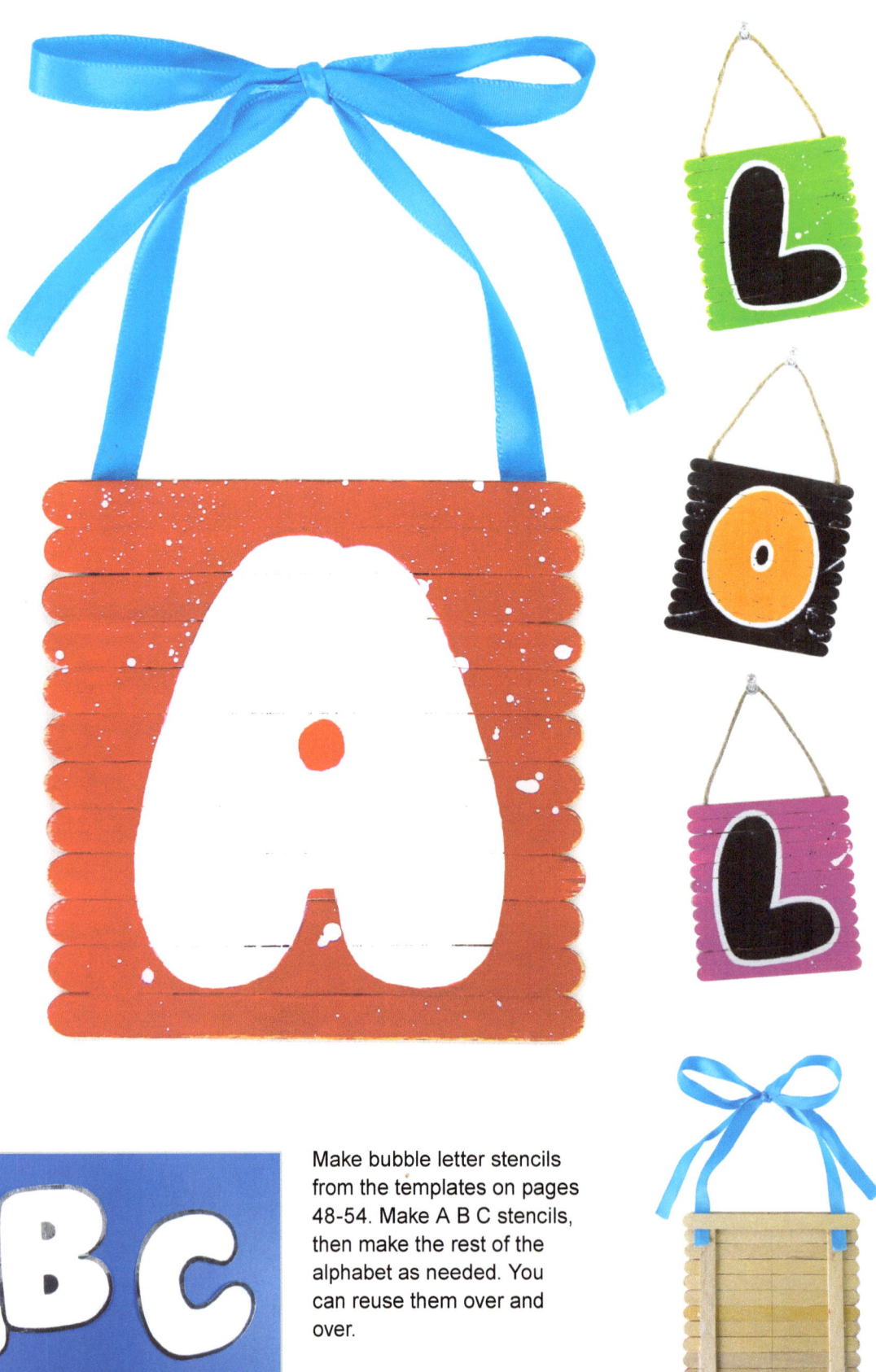

Make bubble letter stencils from the templates on pages 48-54. Make A B C stencils, then make the rest of the alphabet as needed. You can reuse them over and over.

BACK VIEW

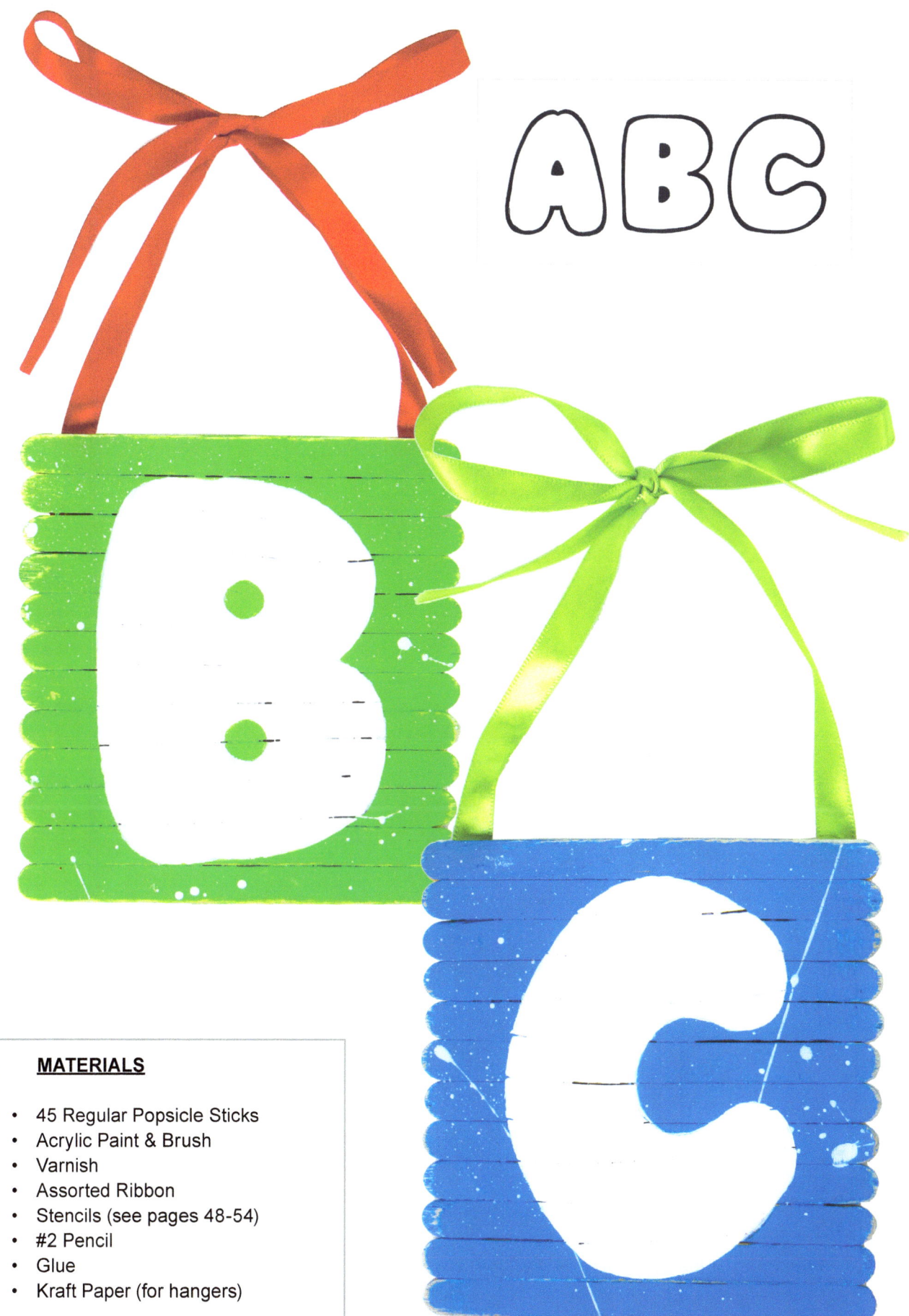

MATERIALS

- 45 Regular Popsicle Sticks
- Acrylic Paint & Brush
- Varnish
- Assorted Ribbon
- Stencils (see pages 48-54)
- #2 Pencil
- Glue
- Kraft Paper (for hangers)

INSTRUCTIONS

STEP 1. Make three plaques with regular popsicle sticks (see page 4).

STEP 2. Make bubble letter stencils A B C. The stencils are part of the standard bubble letter alphabet templates found on pages 48-54. The instructions to make the stencils are located on page 10.

STEP 3. Trace the stencils A B C onto the wood plaques (see page 11).

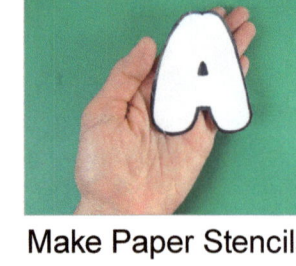

Make Paper Stencils

STEP 4. Paint the letters first with a coat of watery white paint.

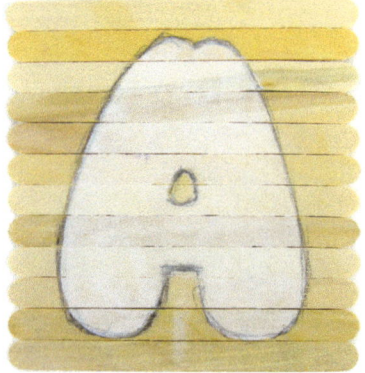 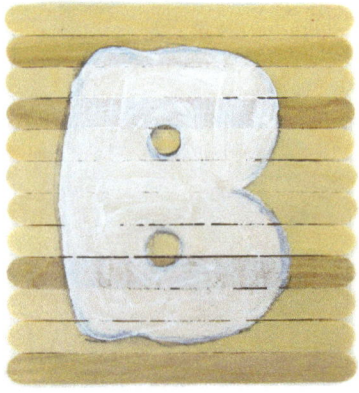 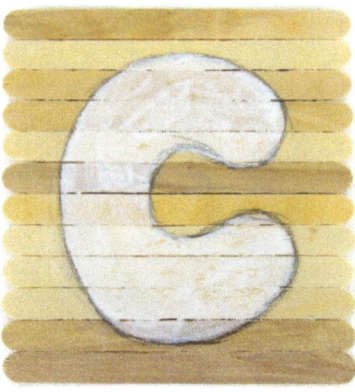

STEP 5. Paint the backgrounds with a coat of watery red, watery green, and watery blue paints.

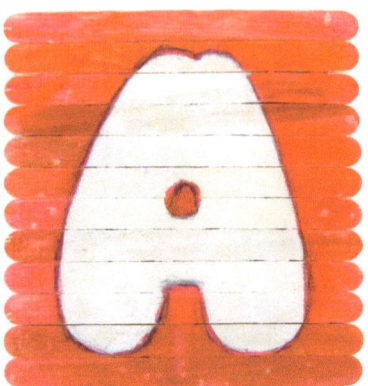 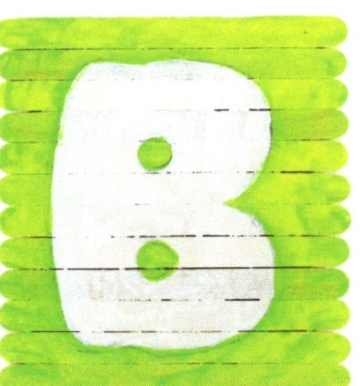 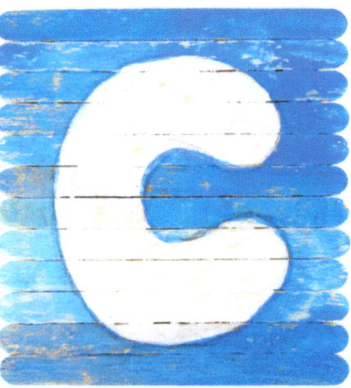

STEP 6. Apply a second coat of paint mixed with very little water. Apply as many coats as needed until your colors are opaque and vibrant. Let the paint dry. Acrylic paint works great on wood.

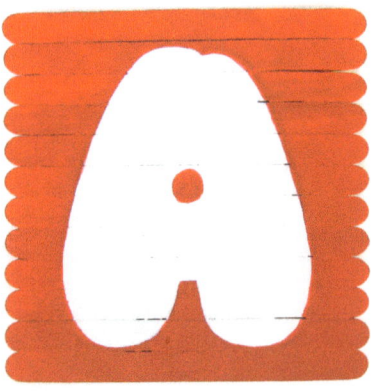 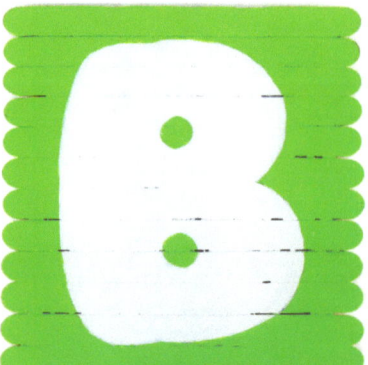 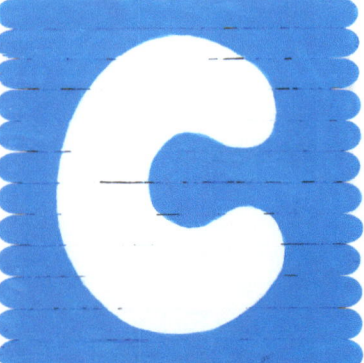

STEP 7. Splash all of the plaques with white paint (see page 17).

STEP 8. When dry, apply a coat of varnish.

STEP 9. Make hangers with brightly colored ribbons and attach to the backs (see page 5).

Now that you know the technique, you can recreate this project with any bubble letters you like. Hang the plaques with brightly colored ribbons or string (see page 5). Or put magnetic tape on the backs (see page 9). Paint a bright white outline around the letters. Why not try a fun word abbreviation (acronym) like one of these below:

LOL: Laugh out loud   FYI: For your information
ILY: I love you   BAE: Babe
BFF: Best friends forever   OMG: Oh my god

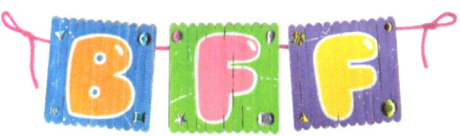

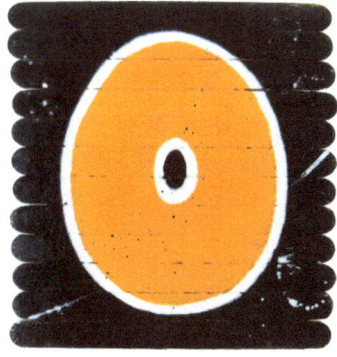

You can add any interesting details to the basic bubble letters once you have your stencils completed. Rotate them and string them together in a group (see pages 8- 9). Paint some gooey paint (or snow) dripping off the tops. Or apply a watery coat of paint to the background to create a tinted look. There are so many options.

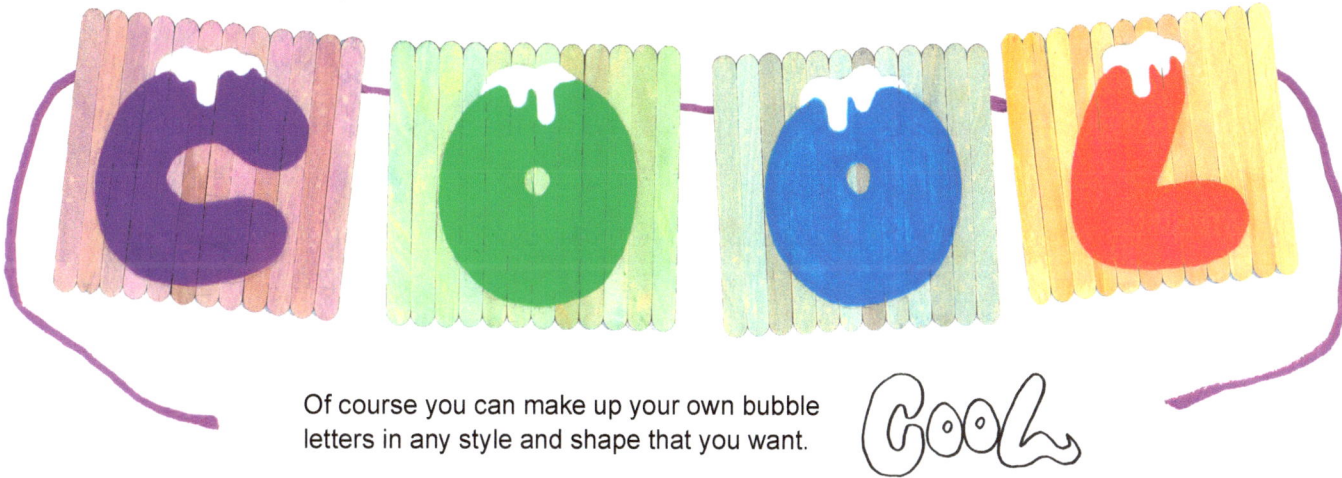

Of course you can make up your own bubble letters in any style and shape that you want.

Add drop shadows to your bubble letters to make them three dimensional. You don't have to make the shadows all just one color either. Try different combinations to see what looks best.

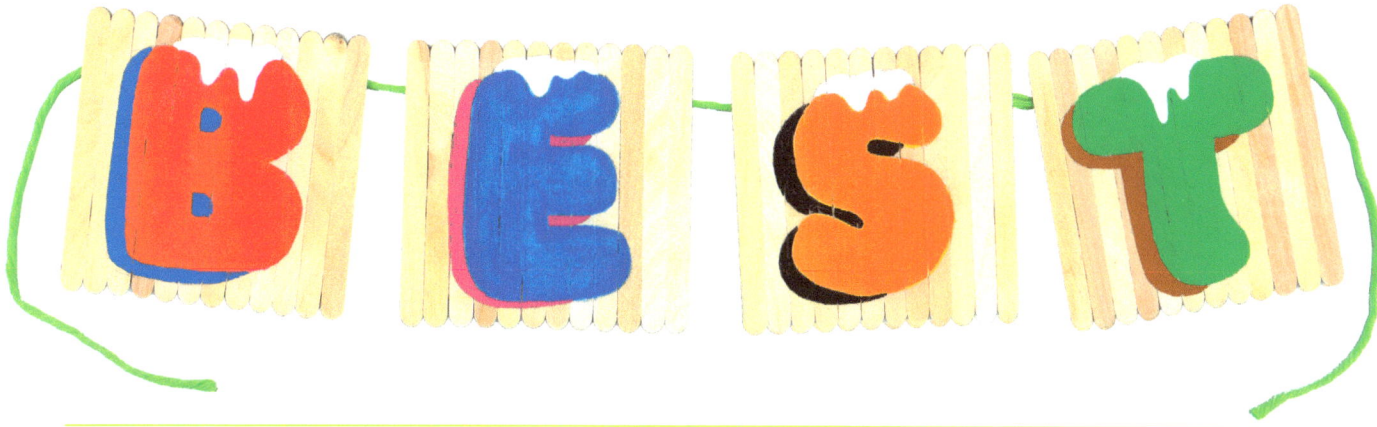

BOO

Make jumbo wall hangings for any occasion. Other ideas you might try:

1) JOY: for the Holidays
2) ILY: for Valentines day

Or you can experiment with just a symbol like one of these:

1) A Jewish star for Hanukkah
2) A clover for St. Patrick's day
3) A flag for July 4th
4) A turkey for Thanksgiving
5) A heart for Valentine's day
6) A bunny for Easter
7) Maracas for Cinco de Mayo
8) Candles for Kwanzaa

Search the Internet for simple images and ideas. Use the stencil technique on page 10 to make your own original stencils and duplicate your wall hanging as many times as you like. Give them to friends or family as gifts.

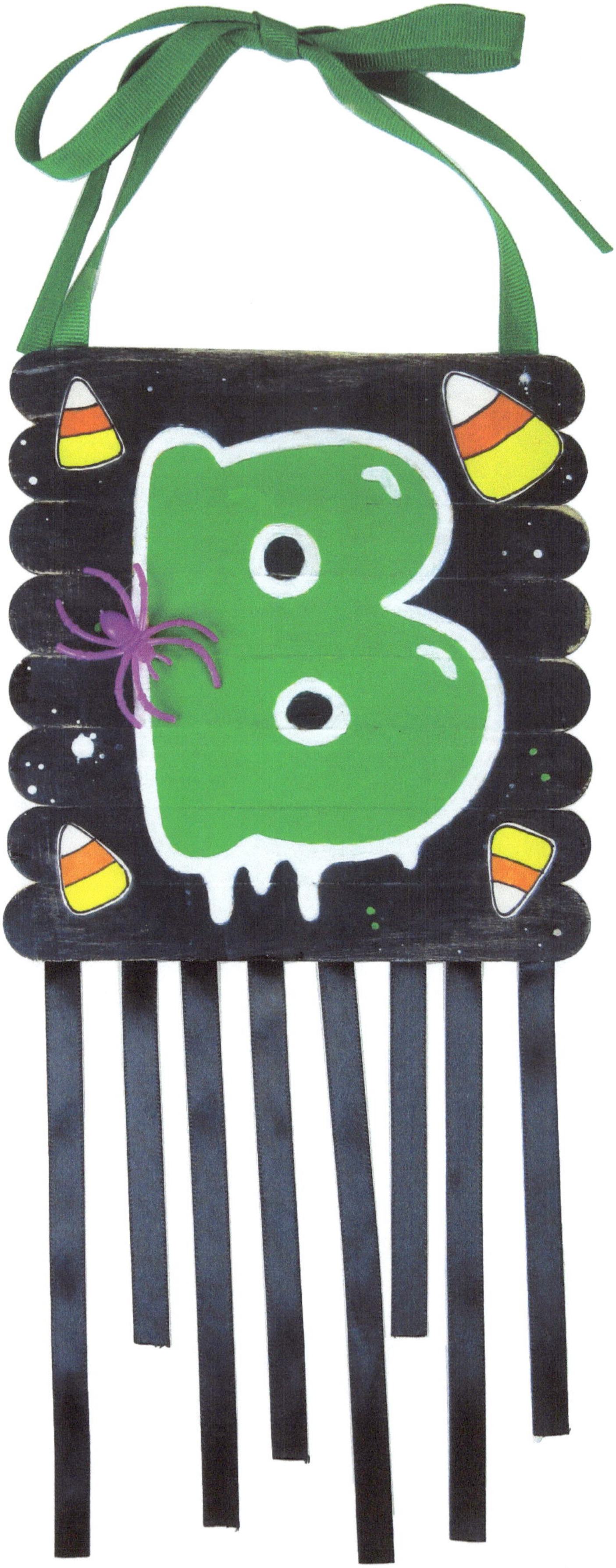

MATERIALS

- 33 Jumbo Popsicle Sticks
- Acrylic Paint & Brush
- Varnish
- Assorted Ribbon
- Stencils (see page 54)
- #2 Pencil
- Good Drawing Paper
- Colored Pencils or Markers
- Plastic ornaments (optional)
- Tacky glue
- Kraft paper (for hangers)

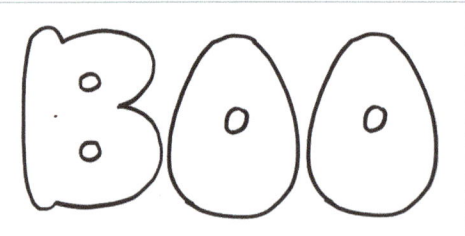

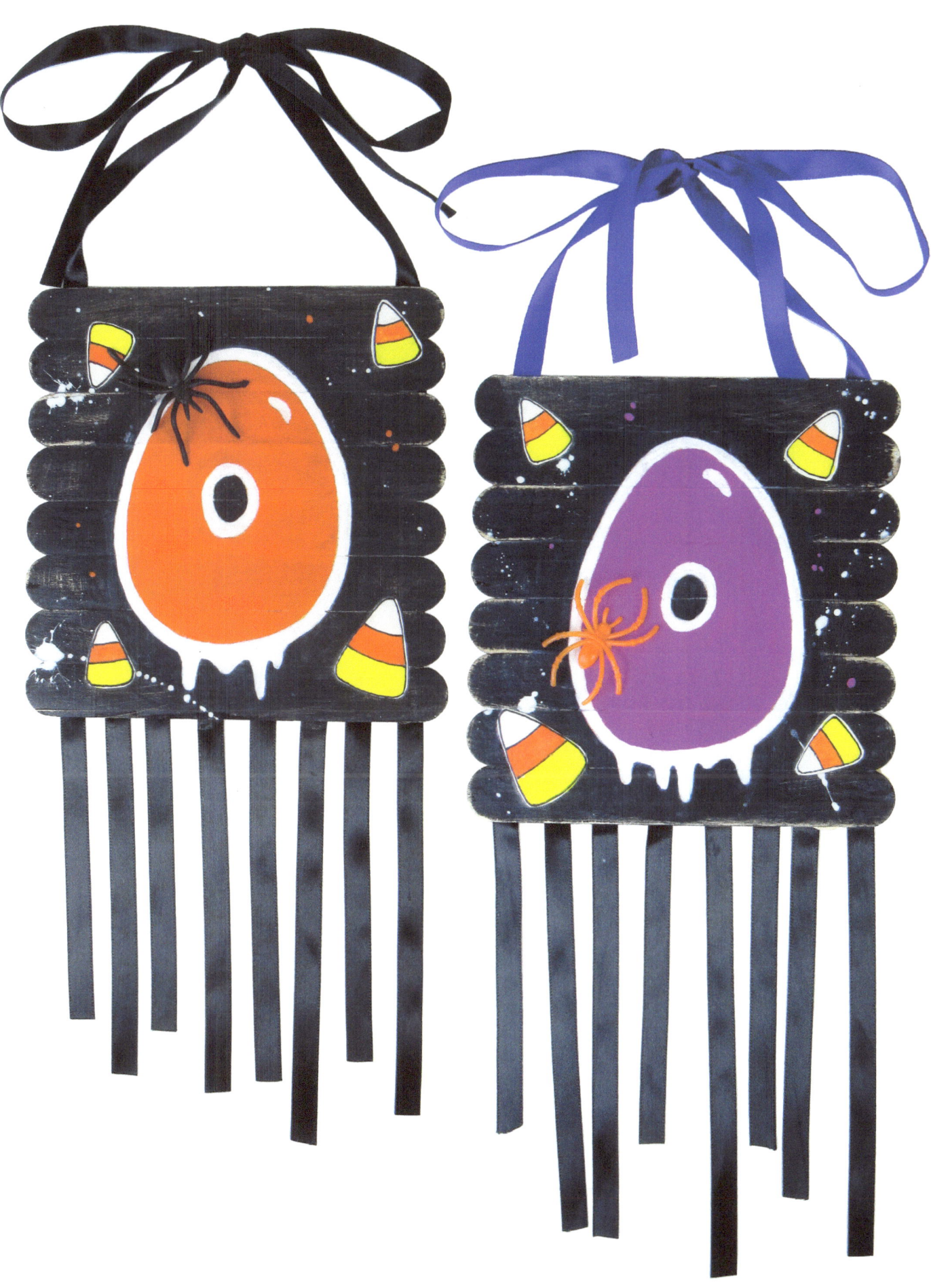

INSTRUCTIONS

STEP 1. Make three jumbo plaques (see page 4).

STEP 2. Make stencils B and O (see page 10 for instructions and page 54 for templates).

STEP 3. Trace the stencils onto the plaques with a pencil.

STEP 4. Paint the backgrounds with a coat of watery black paint.

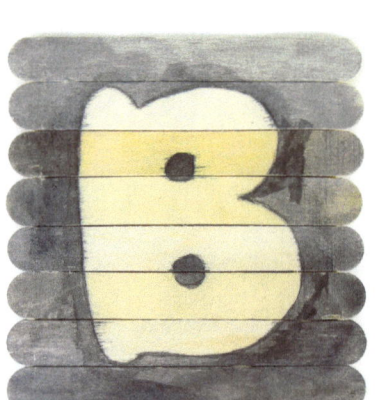 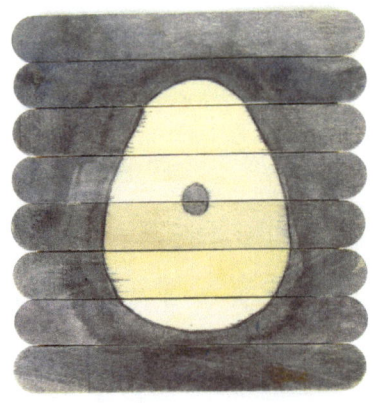 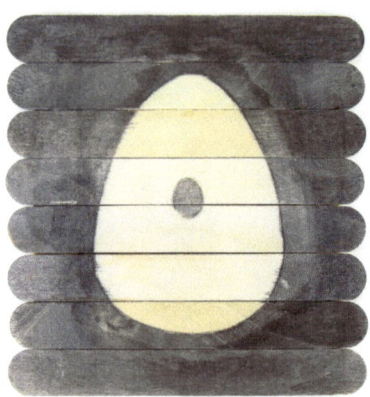

STEP 5. Paint the letters with watery coats of green, orange, and purple paints.

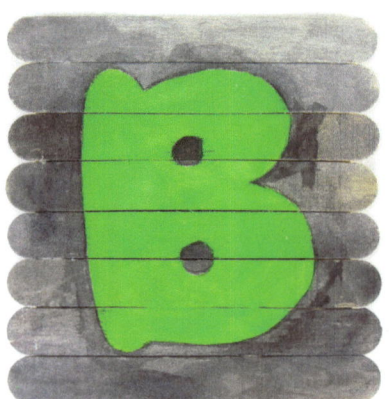 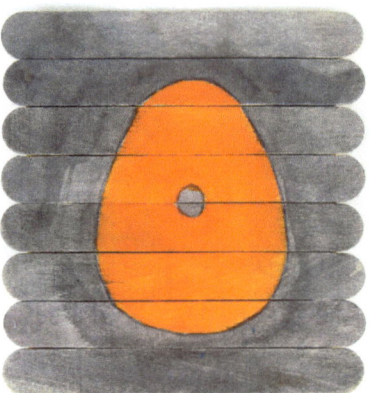 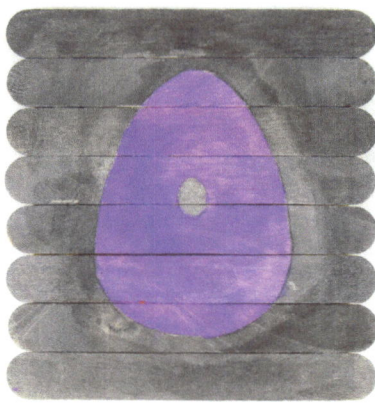

STEP 6. Apply a second coat of all paint colors mixed with very little water. Apply as many coats as needed until your colors look really sharp and vibrant. Let the plaques dry.

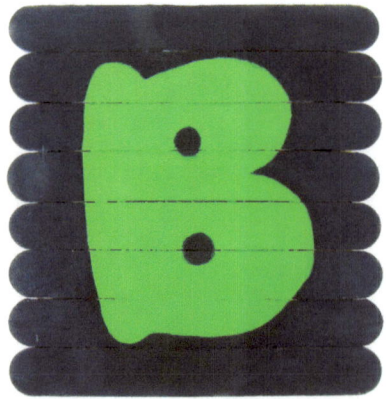 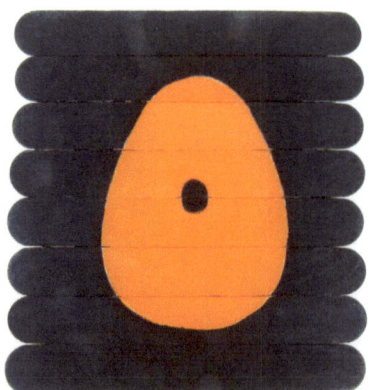 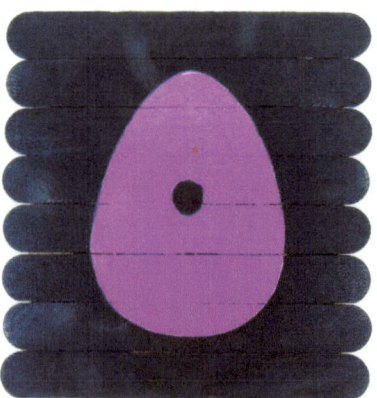

POPSICLE-STICK-GRAFFITI / NUMBER THREE

STEP 7. With a tiny brush, outline the edges of the letters with white paint. Paint drips on the bottoms and highlights inside the letters. Splatter with small drops of white, orange, green and purple paint (see pages 22-23).

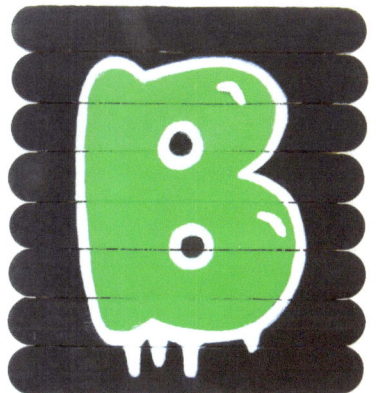 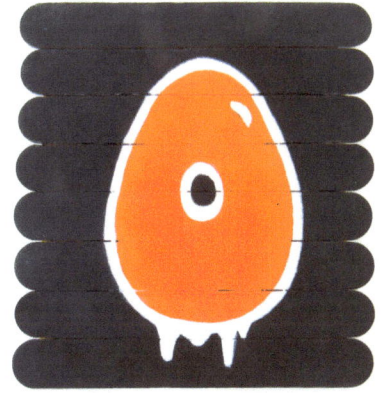 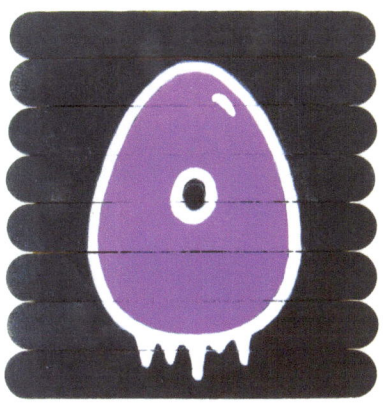

STEP 8. OPTIONAL: When dry, lightly distress the paint with a small piece of sandpaper so some of the wood shows through at the edges (see page 16). Apply varnish to each plaque, one color at a time.

STEP 9. Cut some ribbon streamers for the bottoms. Glue them onto jumbo popsicle sticks with thick tacky glue. Turn the plaques over to the back and glue the sticks with streamers to the bottoms. Let dry.

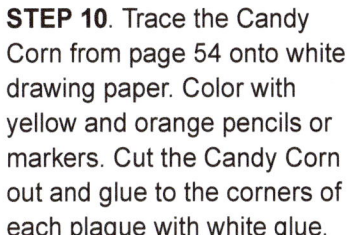

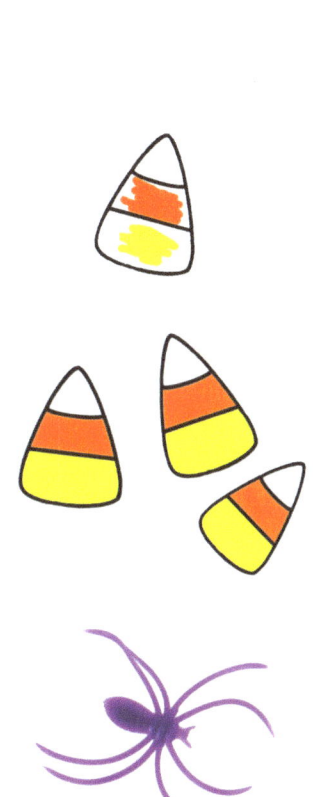

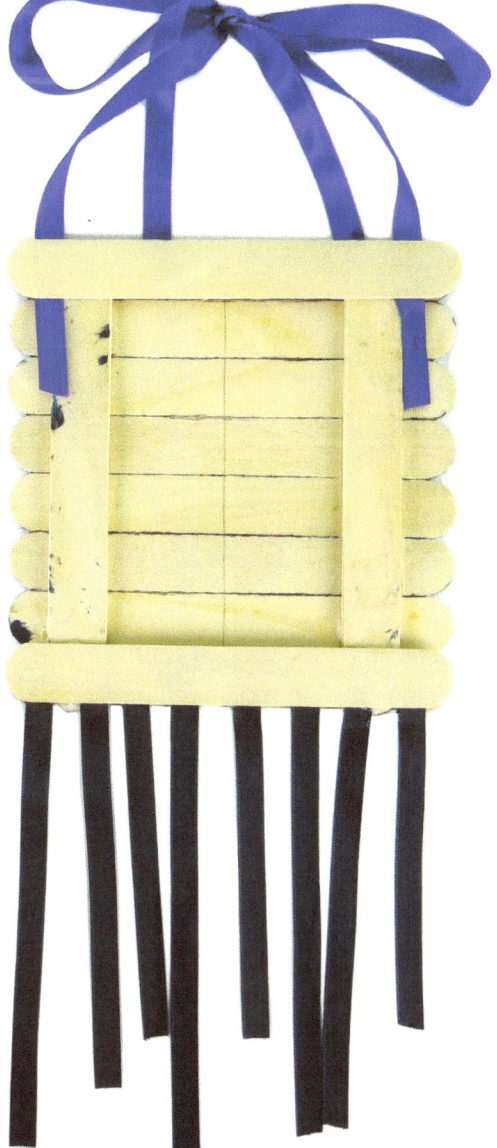

STEP 10. Trace the Candy Corn from page 54 onto white drawing paper. Color with yellow and orange pencils or markers. Cut the Candy Corn out and glue to the corners of each plaque with white glue.

STEP 11. Glue on plastic spiders or any other ornaments with thick tacky glue. Let dry.

STEP 12. Attach ribbons for the hangers (see page 5).

BACK VIEW

PARTY

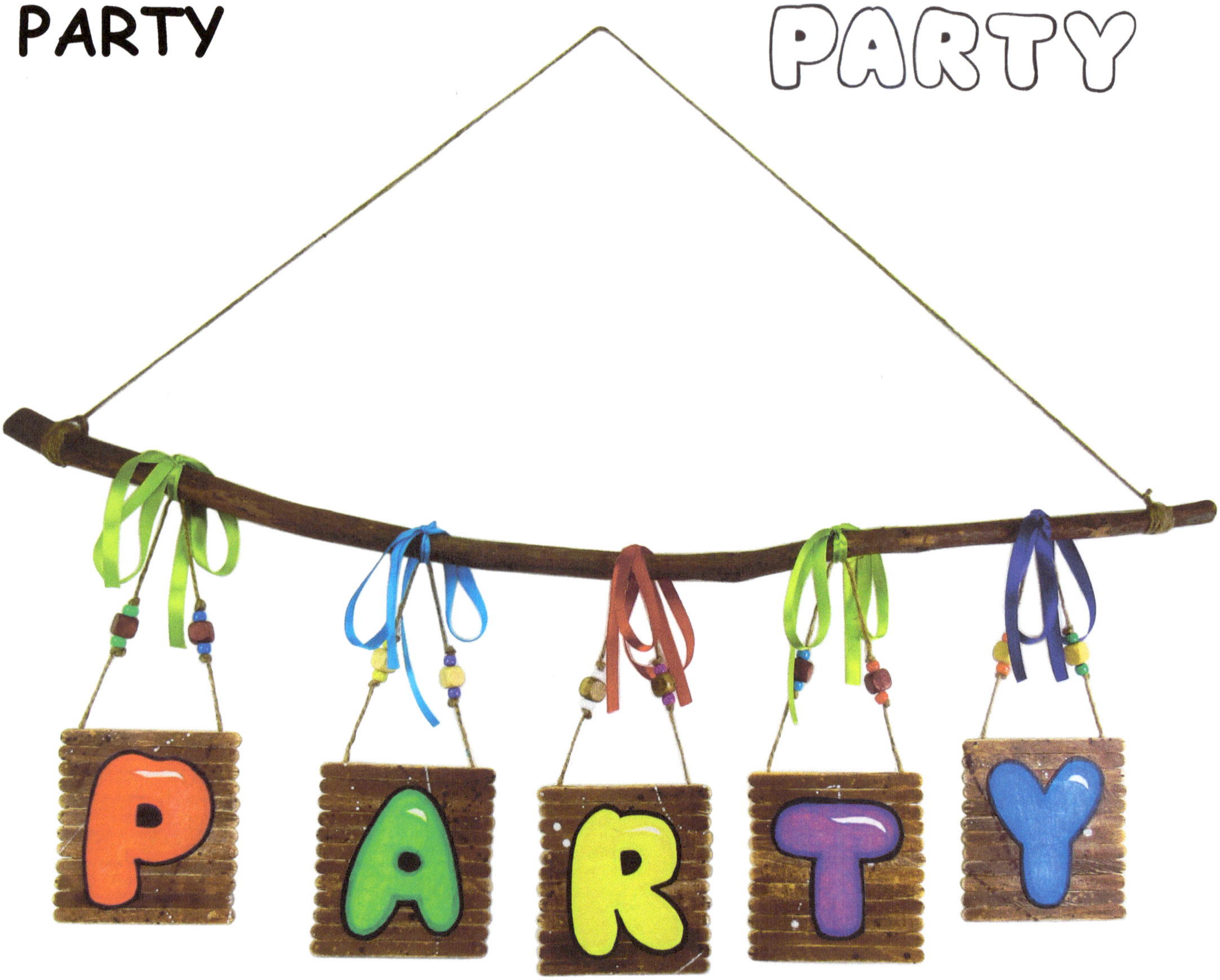

PARTY

MATERIALS

- 75 Regular Popsicle Sticks
- Acrylic Paint & Brush
- Varnish
- Assorted Ribbon
- Stencils (pages 48-54)
- #2 Pencil & Eraser
- Good Drawing Paper
- Twine or String
- Beads
- Black Sharpie
- Glue
- Mod Podge
- Crayons or Colored Pencils
- Tree Branch

A tree branch is a great way to hang multiple plaques with only one tack or push pin on your wall. If you don't have a branch you can use a wood dowel or any other type of stick. Even a clothing hanger can work. This wall hanging is made with paper cutouts (see pages 12-13). You can make this or any other word you like using the templates on pages 48-54.

Some other word ideas you might like to try: ALOHA, PEACE, LOVE, DANCE, SWEET, FRIEND, TRAVEL, EXPLORE, MOM, DAD, HAPPY. You can modify the bubble letters and change the way they look. These ALOHA letters are drawn extra fat and bubbly. A Hawaiian flower is substituted for the letter O. I copied the flower from a photo on the Internet.

 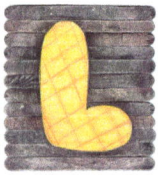  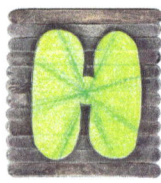 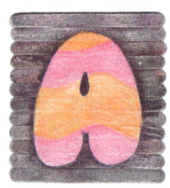

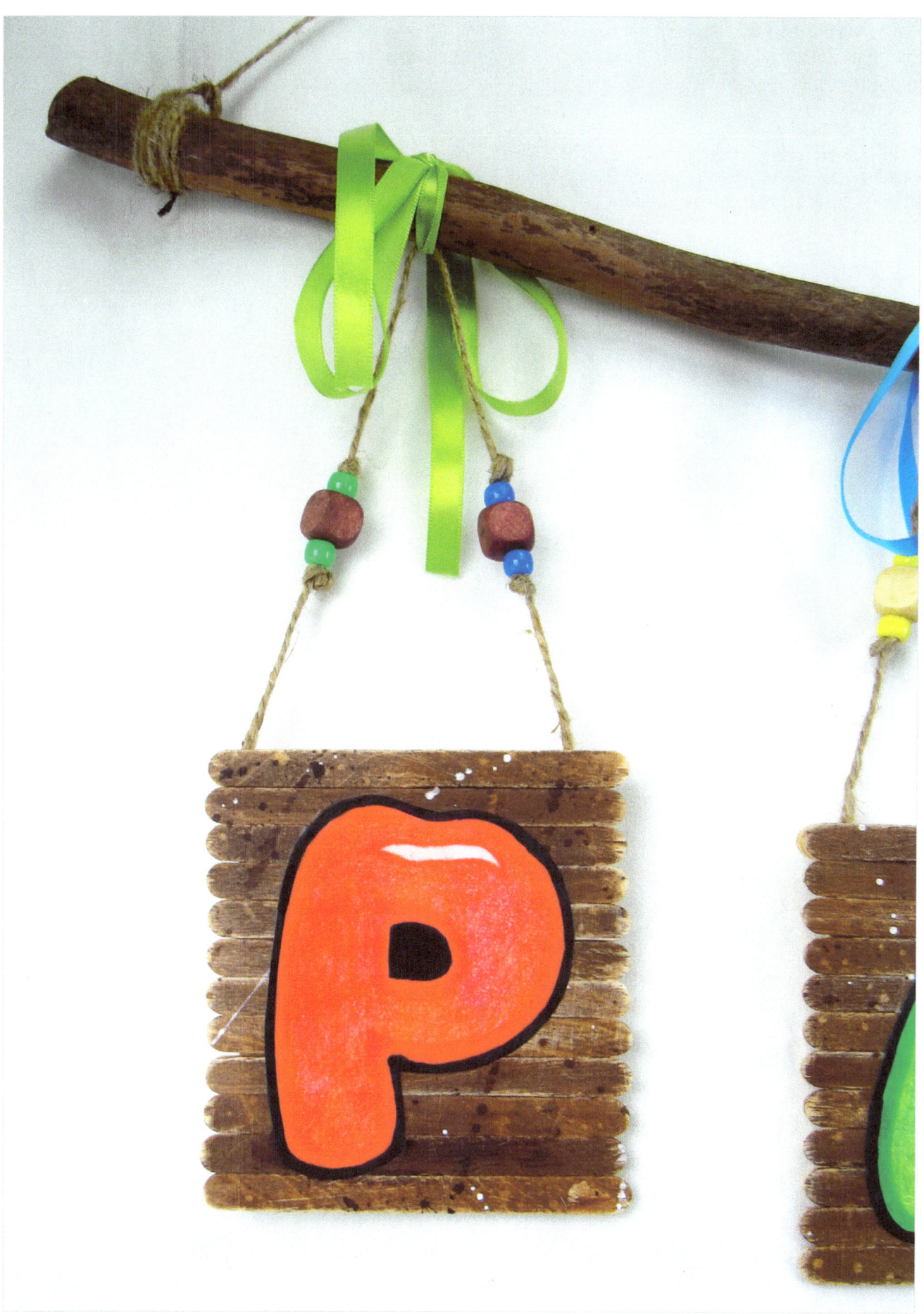

You can leave the wood branch natural or paint it with brightly colored acrylic paint. I like to paint my branches with watery brown paint to even out the color. If you are working with a wood dowel, paint it or leave it unpainted. Apply a coat or two of varnish.

TREE BRANCH
STEP 1. Find a long, fairly straight tree branch. Clean it will some disinfectant cleaner and a rag. Let it dry.
STEP 2. Remove any loose bark and sand down any off rough edges with a piece of sandpaper.
STEP 3. Paint and varnish, or just varnish. Use any brand of water-based varnish, shiny or flat.

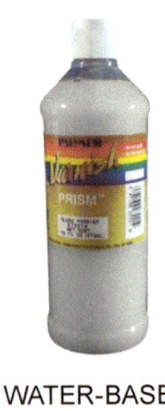

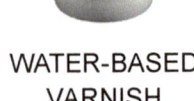

WATER-BASED
VARNISH

1

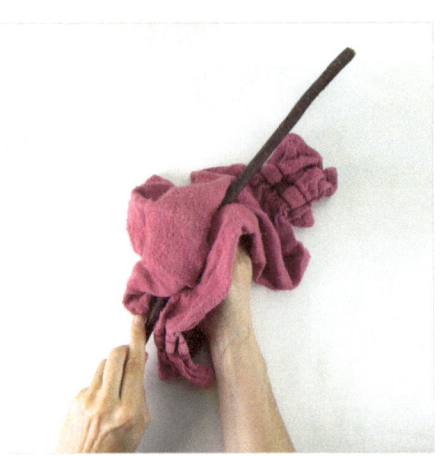

2

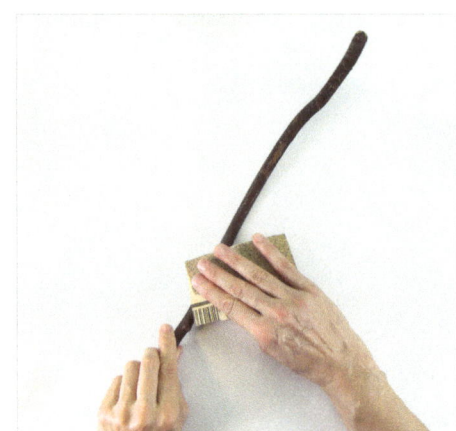

PLAQUES

STEP 1. Make five plaques with regular size popsicle sticks (see page 4).

STEP 2. Mix up some brown paint with water in a small container. With a large brush, apply a coat of this watery paint to all five plaques. Apply several coats. Let the paint dry. The color I used is called Burnt Umber, but you can use any brown paint that you have.

STEP 3. Optional: Rub the edges of the popsicle sticks with sandpaper to create a distressed look if desired (see page 16).

STEP 4. Splatter the plaques with white and dark brown paint (see page 17). Put aside to dry.

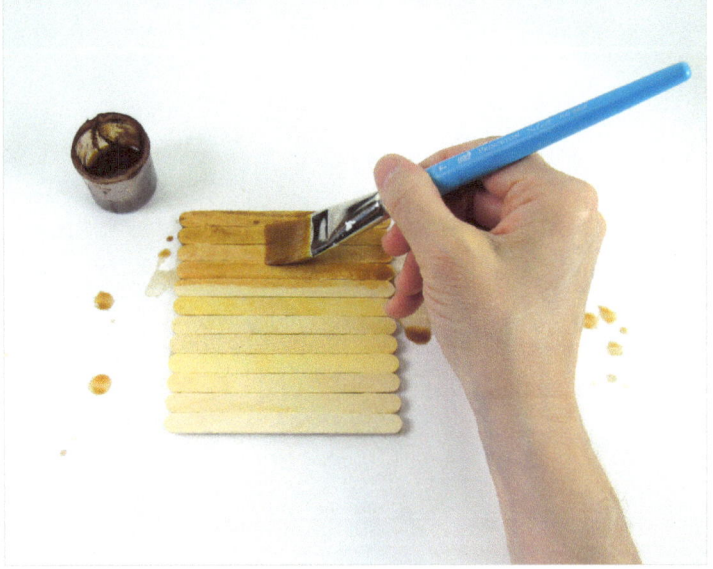

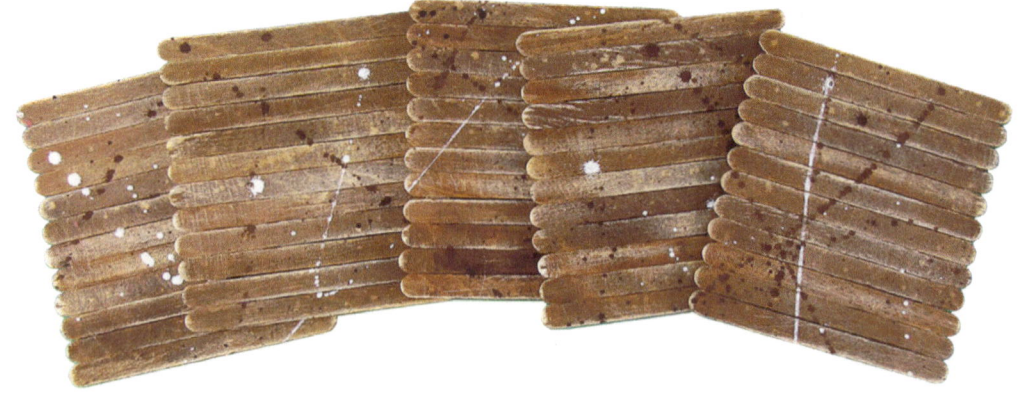

STEP 5. Make bubble letter stencils from the templates on pages 48-54 (see page 10 for details).

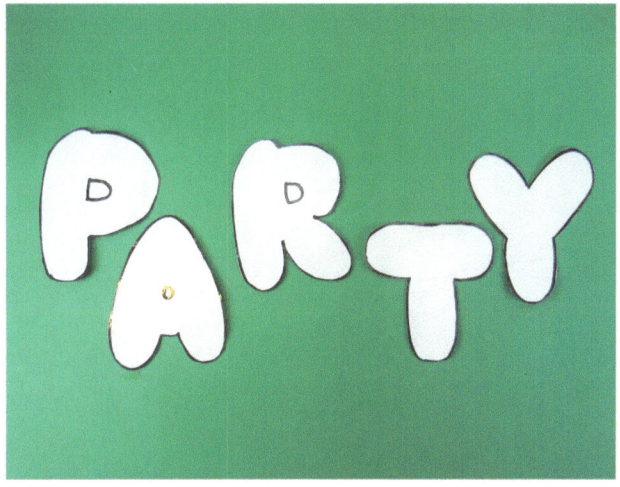

STEP 6. With a pencil, trace the stencils onto a piece of good quality drawing paper.

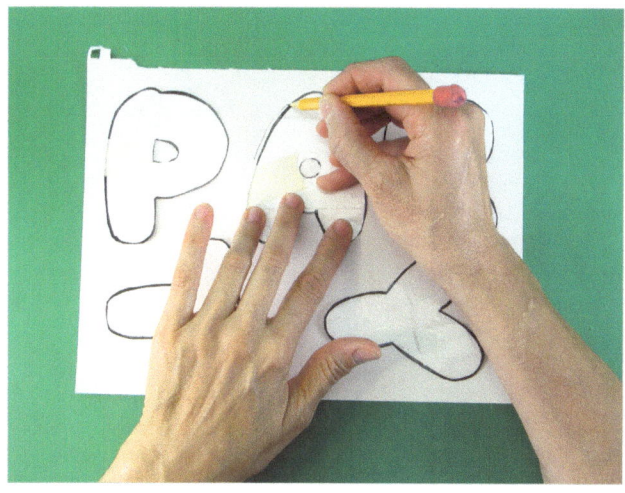

STEP 7. Draw thick outlines over the pencil lines with a black Sharpie. Erase the pencil lines.

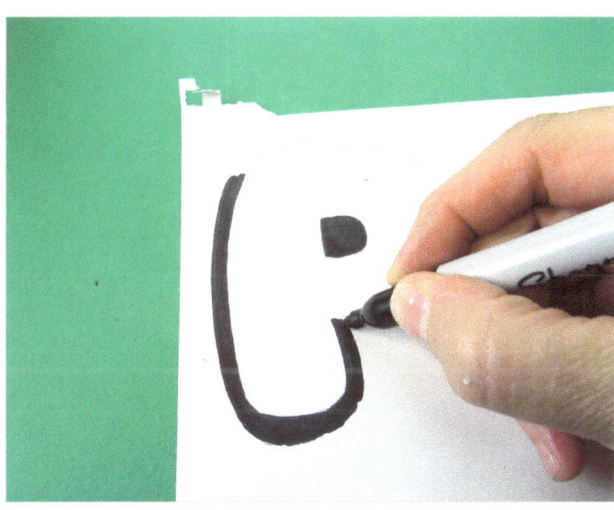

STEP 8. Color in the bubble letters any way you like with colored pencils, magic markers, or crayons.

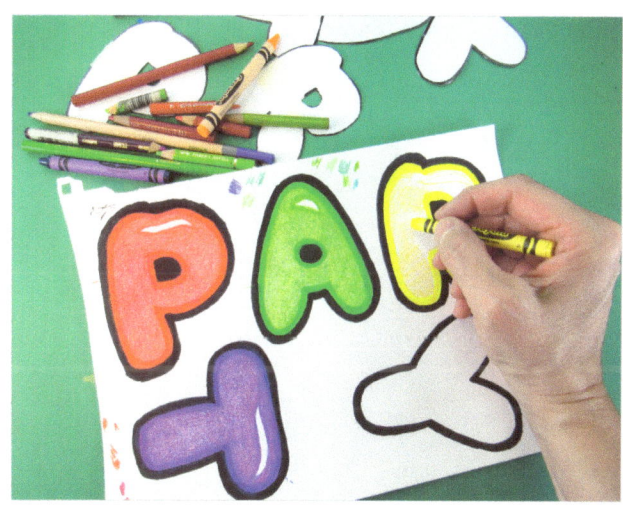

STEP 9. Optional: If the paper is light-weight, coat the back with Mod Podge (see page 12).

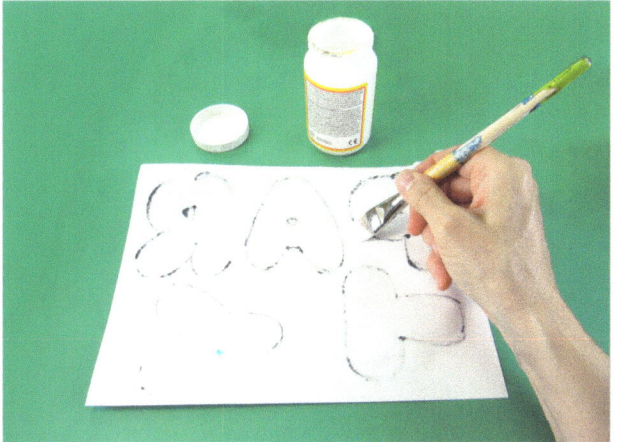

STEP 10. When the Mod Podge is dry, cut the letters out. Include the black outlines on your cutouts.

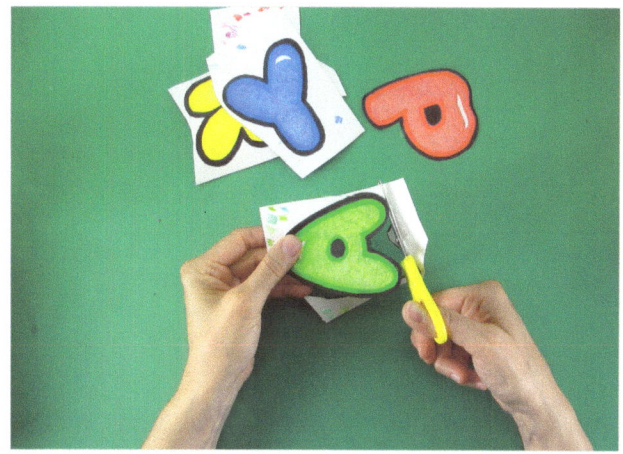

STEP 11. Spread glue evenly on the backs of the letters. Glue the letters in your desired locations onto the plaques.

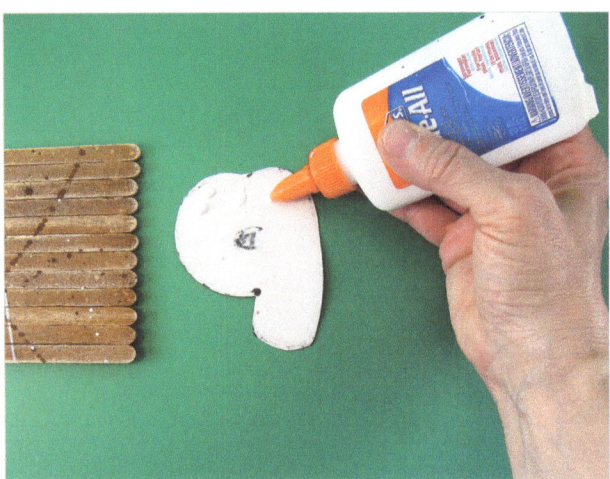

STEP 12. Lay a piece of clear cellophane or plastic wrap over the letters and press down firmly. Remove the plastic. Carefully wipe away any excess glue.

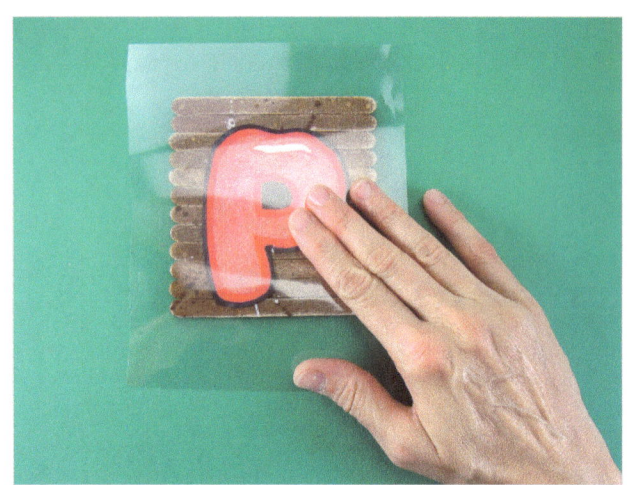

STEP 13. Apply a coat of varnish, first to the letters, then to the backgrounds. When dry, apply a second coat evenly across the whole front.

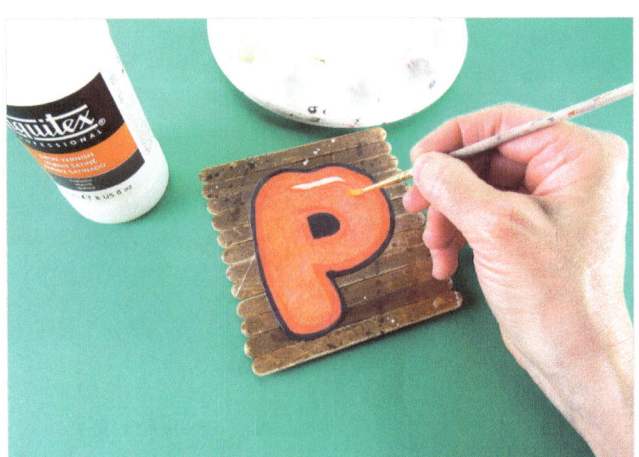

STEP 14. Thread some beads onto pieces of string and make them into hangers (see page 5). Attach the hangers to the back of plaques with thick tacky glue.

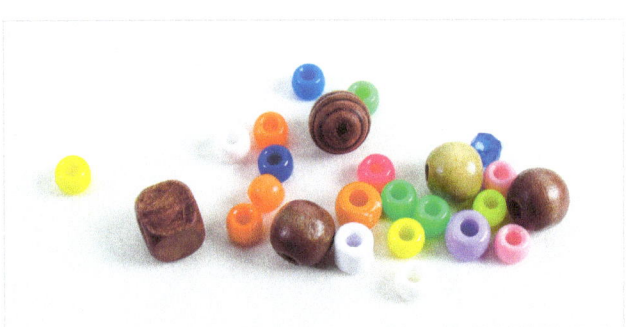

You can use any kind of beads: plastic, wood, glass.

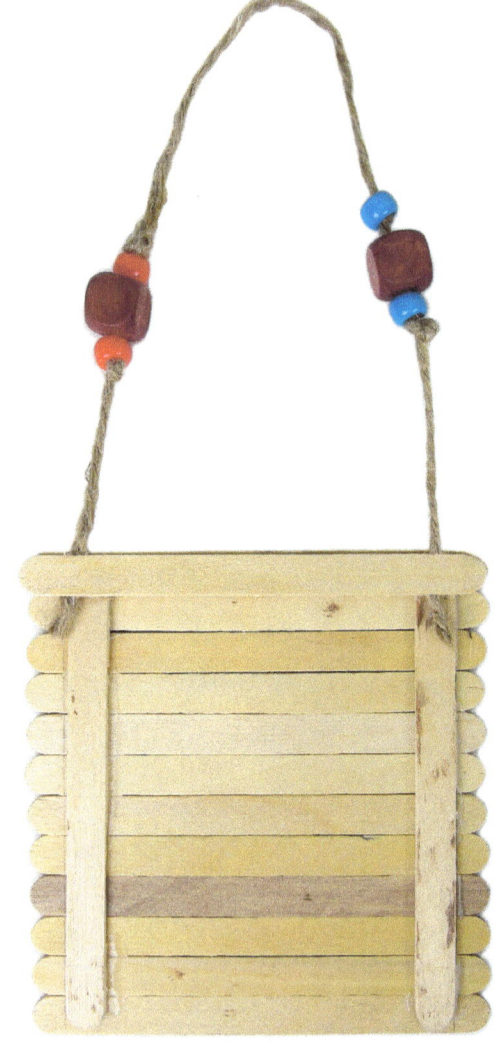

BACK VIEW

STEP 15. Wrap the ends of a long piece of string around each end of the branch to hang.

STEP 16. Complete all the plaques and tie them onto the branch with brightly colored ribbon or string.

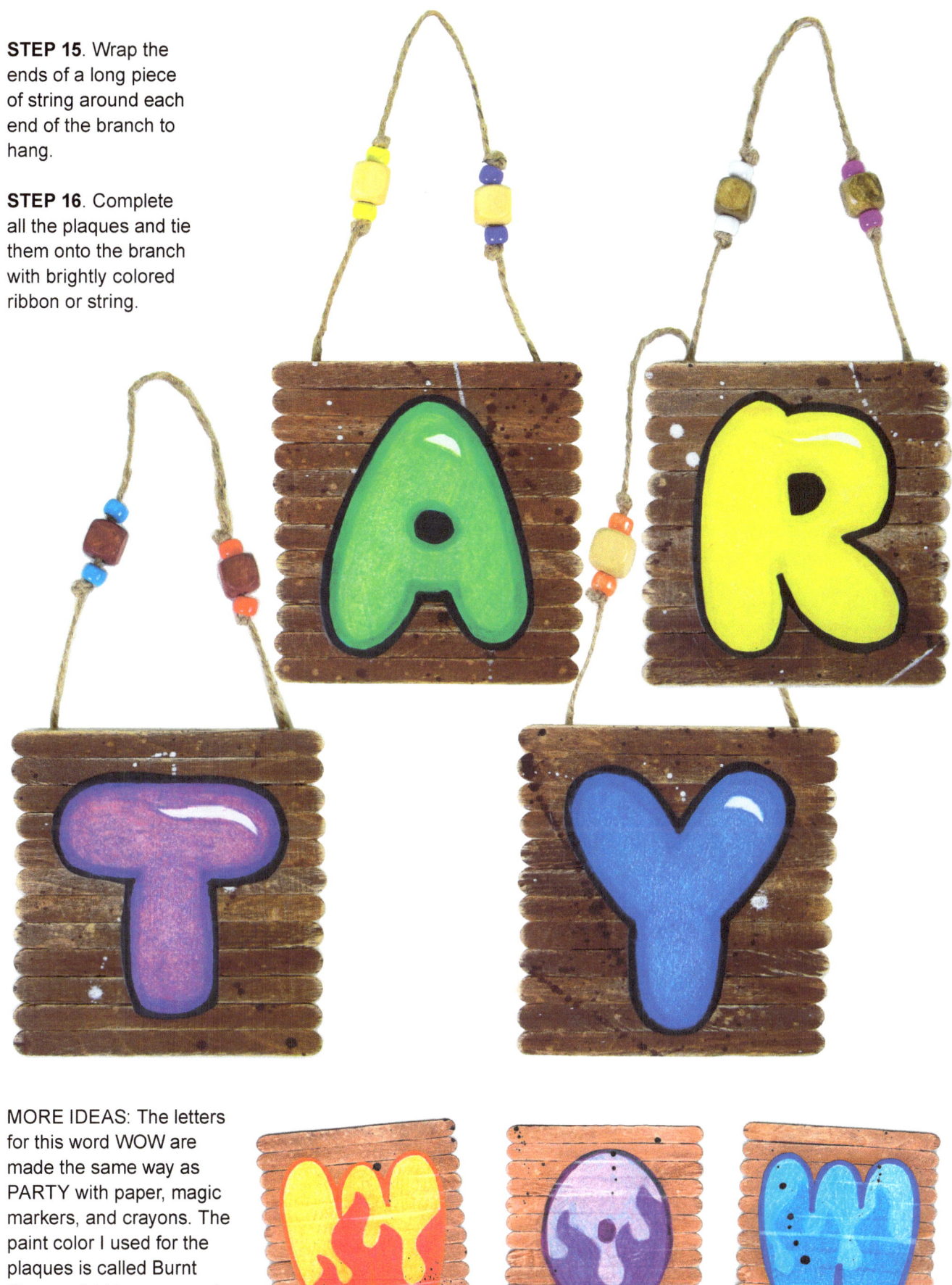

MORE IDEAS: The letters for this word WOW are made the same way as PARTY with paper, magic markers, and crayons. The paint color I used for the plaques is called Burnt Sienna. Add hangers and tie them to a branch with brightly colored ribbon.

SMILE

Create a stylish verticle wall hanging. String as many letters together as you like. You just need strong string or twine to hold the piece together because it can get a bit heavy.

To make this SMILE design, you have options. Use either the standard bubble letter templates on pages 48-54, or the special templates located on pages 55-56. The special templates are a bit more squared-off at the tips. Feel free to alter the letters however you like. There is no right or wrong way to draw bubble letters.

Construct your stencils and use them to make paper cutouts (see pages 12-13). Decorate the cutouts with exciting patterns in your choice of bright colors. I used magic markers and colored pencils in this example. Notice how festive and vibrant the finished wall hanging looks. Just like real graffiti!

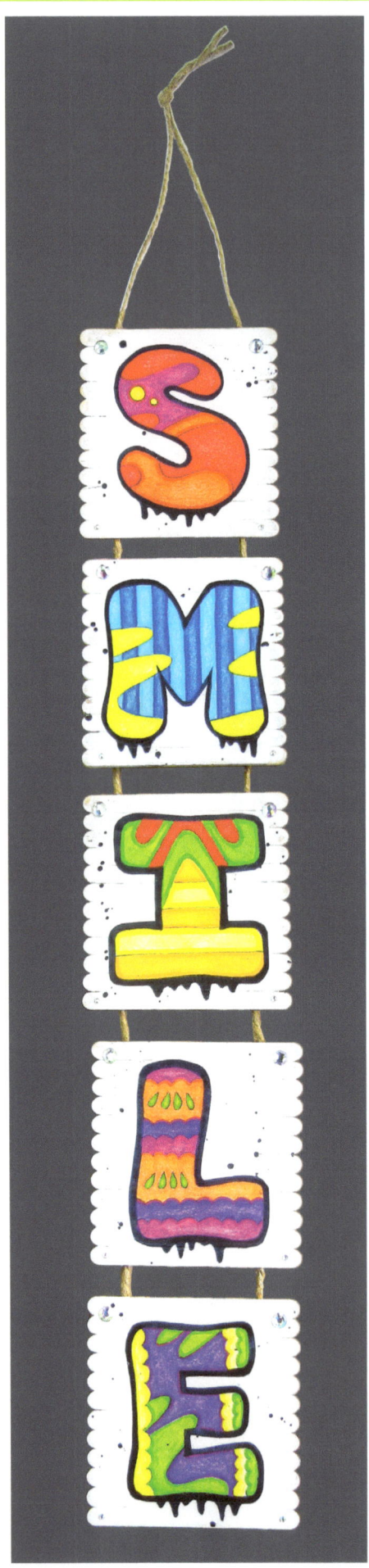

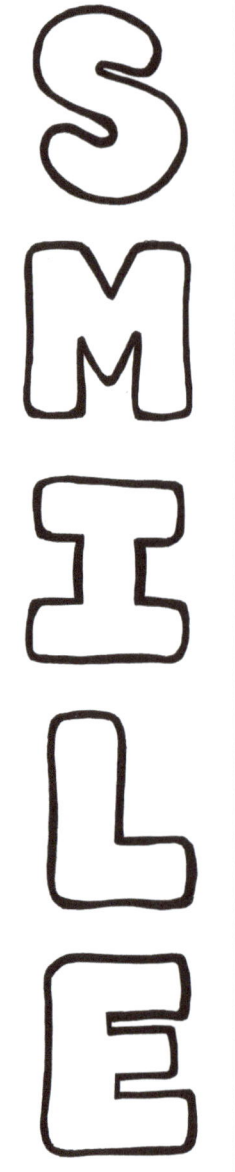

You can also make these bubble letter plaques with magnetic tape on the back (see page 9).

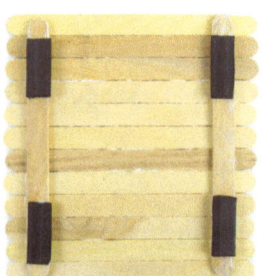

MATERIALS

- 80 Regular Popsicle Sticks
- Stencils
- #2 Pencil & Eraser
- Good Drawing Paper
- Twine or Strong String
- Black Sharpie
- Glue
- Mod Podge
- Colored Pencils
- Acrylic Paint & Brush
- Varnish
- Clear Plastic Cellophane
- Rhinestones

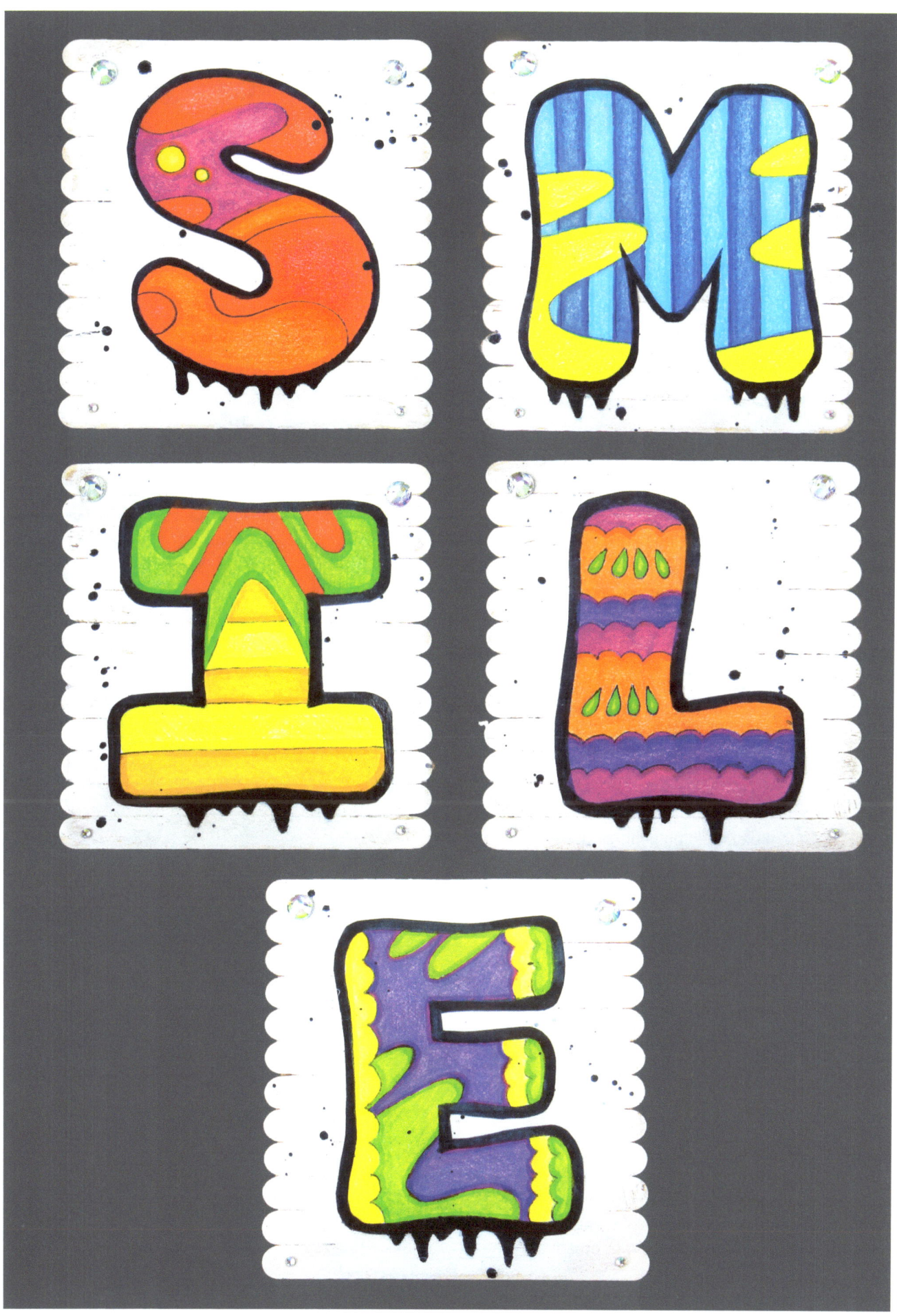

INSTRUCTIONS

STEP 1. Make five plaques with regular size sticks (see page 4). Paint them with white paint and let them dry. Splash with tiny dots of black paint.

STEP 2. Use the bubble letter templates (see pages 48-54 or pages 55-56) to make stencils (see page 10).

STEP 3. With a pencil, trace the stencils onto a piece of good drawing paper.

STEP 4. Go around the outlines with a black Sharpie marker and erase the pencil lines.

STEP 5. Color the letters with colored pencils, crayons, or magic markers in patterns and colors of your choice.

STEP 6. If the paper is thin, put a coat of Mod Podge on the back and let it dry.

STEP 7. Cut the letters out. Include the black outlines on your cutouts.

STEP 8. Glue the cutouts onto the plaques in your desired locations.

STEP 9. Lay a piece of clear plastic cellophane or plastic wrap on top and press the letters down firmly. Remove the plastic.

STEP 10. Paint in little black drips on the bottoms of the bubble letters with a small brush.

STEP 11. Apply varnish with the small brush. Coat each section of color separately so the colors don't bleed into each other. When dry, apply a second coat of varnish over the whole surface with a larger brush.

1

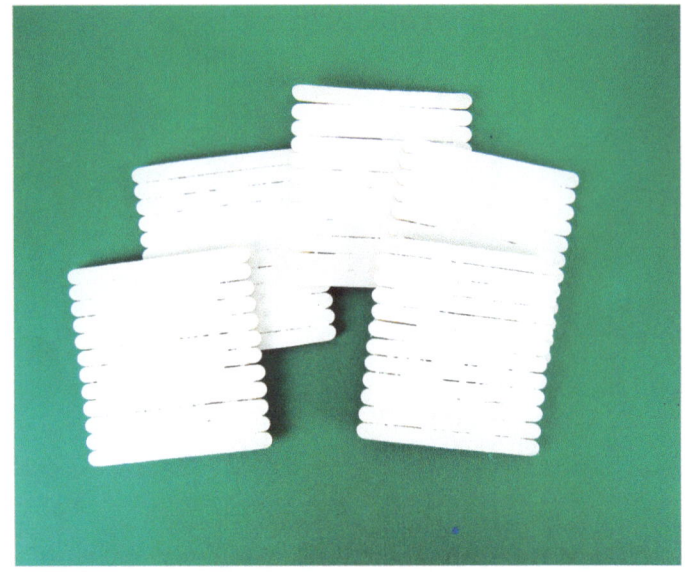

3

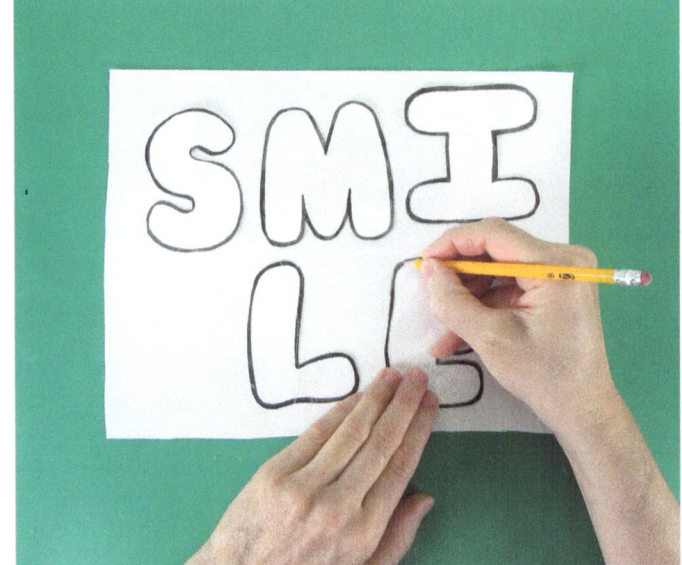

5

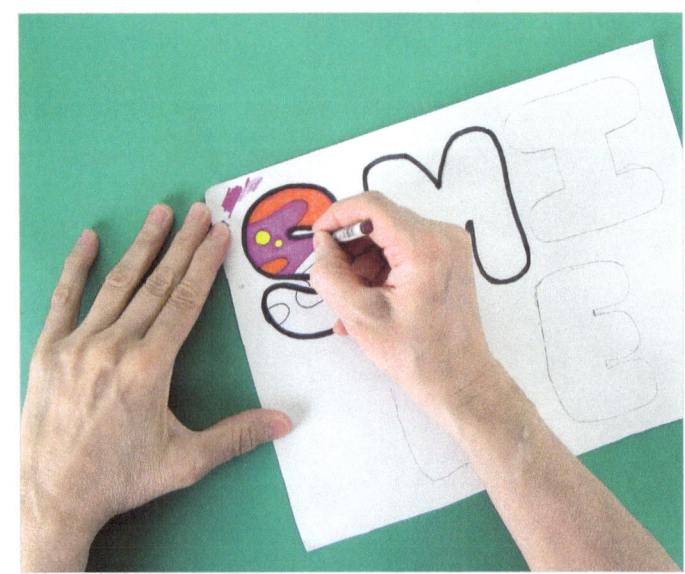

7

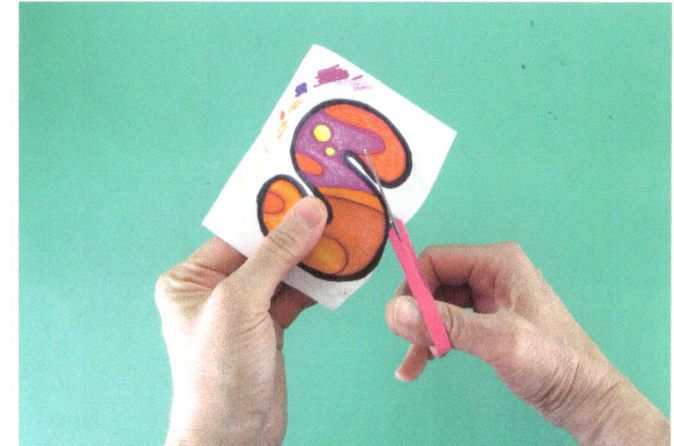

8

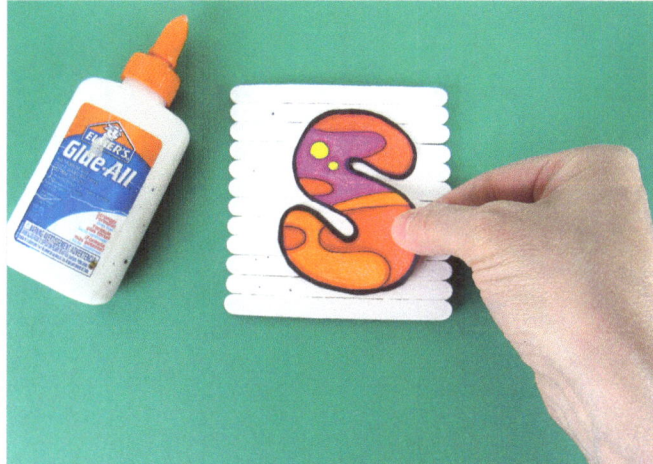

10

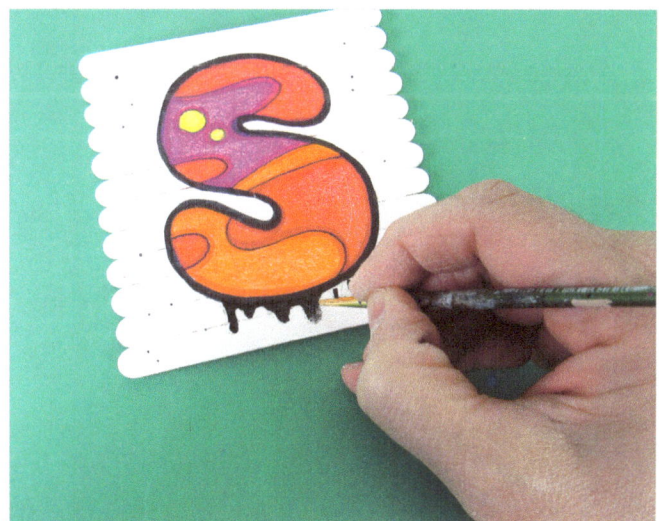

STEP 12. Glue on rhinestones in the corners. You can splatter with a tiny bit more black paint if desired.

STEP 13. Attach strings to the back of the plaques for mounting on the wall (see page 8). Do not attempt to hang the piece until the glue has dried thoroughly.

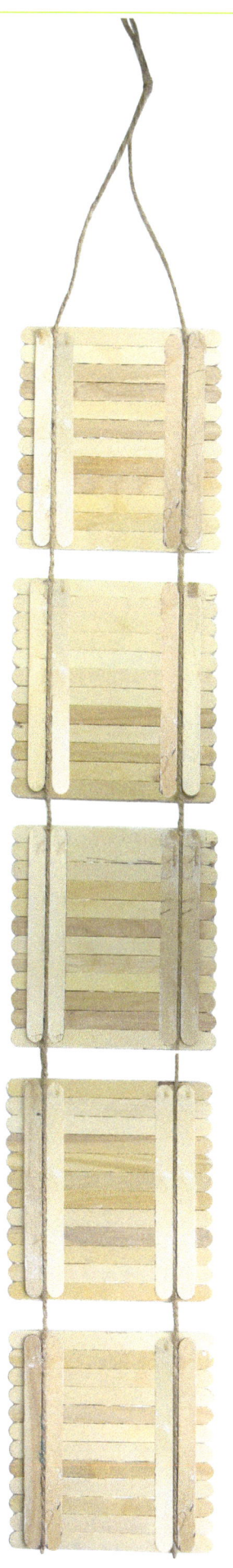

BACK
VIEW

THROWIES

A Throwie is a quickly drawn bubble letter outline usually consisting of one or two colors. These examples are just random letters I picked to show you the technique. Try inventing your own bubble letter throwie in a similar style. Use either a short nickname or just your initials. Complete your throwie wall hanging with a ribbon, string, or magnetic tape. There are no stencils in this book for throwies, but the letters are drawn the same way as any other bubble letters (see page 15).

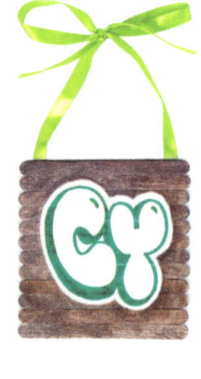
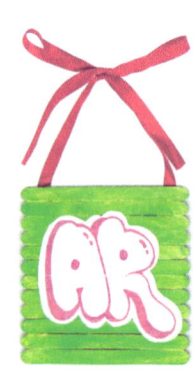

STEP 1. Draw two bubble letters. The edges can overlap.

STEP 2. Draw a drop shadow on one side of the letters.

STEP 3. Draw an outline around the two letters to make one shape.

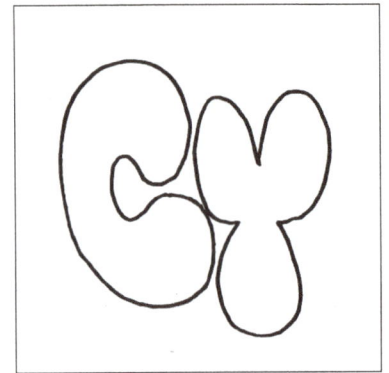
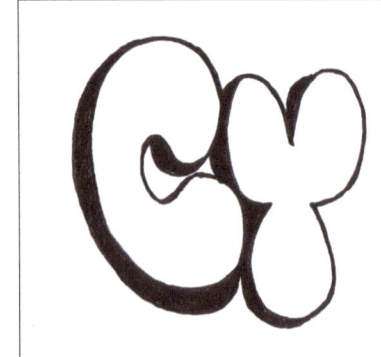
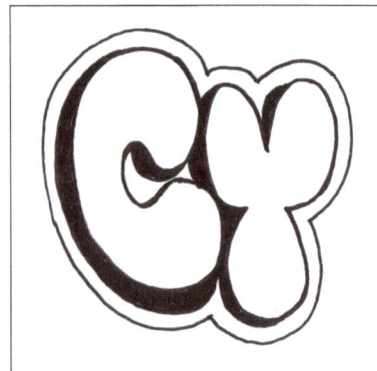

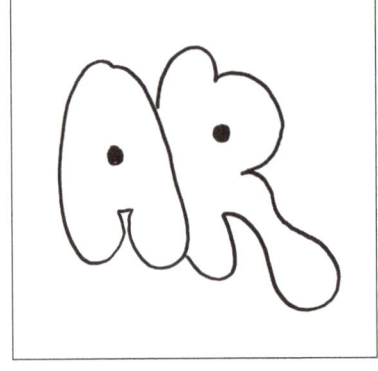
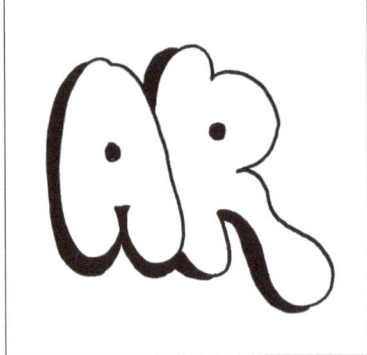
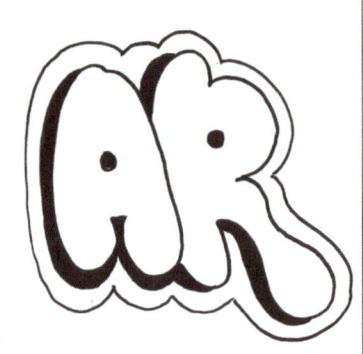

THROWIE PAPER CUTOUT

STEP 1. On a piece of good drawing paper, draw a throwie with any two letters following the steps above.
STEP 2. Cut out the throwie and glue it onto a plaque.
STEP 3. Apply a coat of varnish.
STEP 4. Attach a hanger.

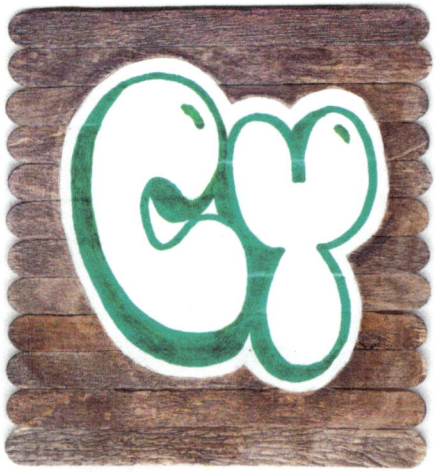
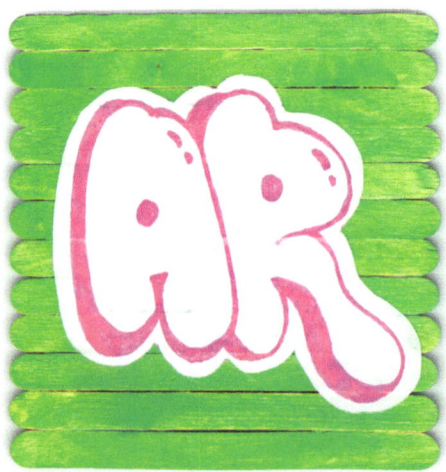

If your throwie has more than two letters or is too big to fit on a regular size plaque, put it on a jumbo plaque. You can paint it directly on the plaque or make a paper cutout. This example below is a paper cutout.

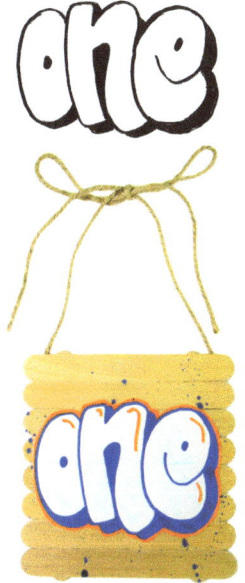

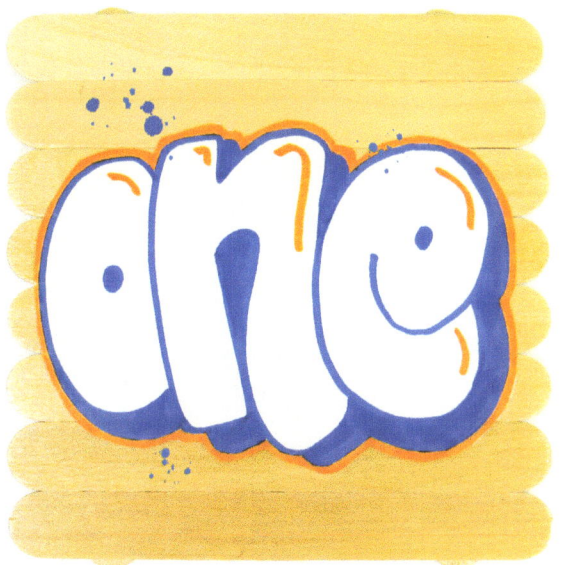

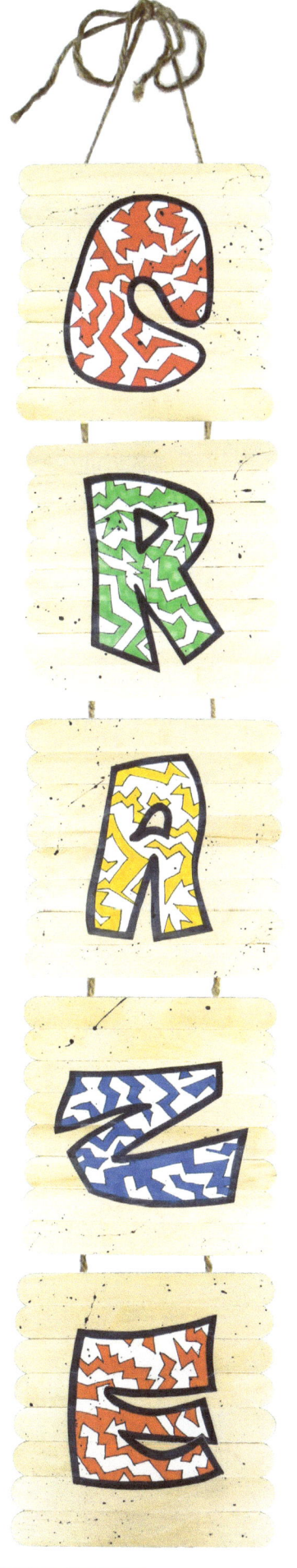

Add your own style, just be sure to make your letters fat and bubbly. Refer to the diagram on page 15 if you need help drawing bubble letters. With practice you will be able to draw your own great throwies.

FREESTYLE

Why not try drawing your own freestyle letters? They can be in any shape and style you want to draw as long as they are outline letters with room inside so you can add color or patterns. No stencils are required!

INSTRUCTIONS

STEP 1. Draw some letters on good quality drawing paper. Size them to fit on either regular or jumbo plaques.
STEP 2. Outline them with a black Sharpie.
STEP 3. Color them in with your choice of magic markers, colored pencils, or crayons.
STEP 4. Optional: Apply a coat of Mod Podge to the back of the paper.
STEP 5. Cut them out.
STEP 6. Glue them onto the plaques.
STEP 7. Varnish them.
STEP 8. Attach a string to hang them up.

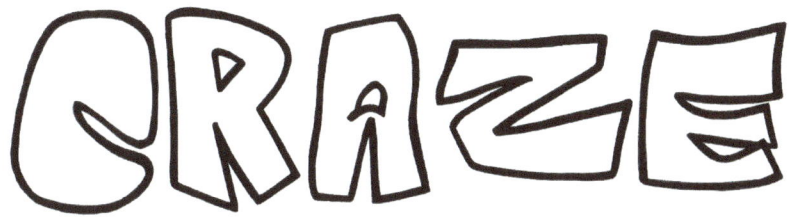

MORE FREESTYLE

INSTRUCTIONS

STEP 1. Make four regular size plaques (see page 4) and paint them red. Put them aside to dry.

STEP 2. Draw some fun, freestyle letters on good quality drawing paper. Add arrows to the ends of the letters.
There are no stencils for these letters. You have to draw them yourself, free-hand.

STEP 3. Color them in with your choice of magic markers, colored pencils, or crayons.

STEP 4. Optional: Apply a coat of Mod Podge to the back of the paper.
This makes the letters easier to handle.

STEP 5. Cut the letters out.

STEP 6. Glue them onto the plaques.

STEP 7. Varnish them.

STEP 8. Glue two wiggly eyes onto the O with thick white glue..

STEP 9. Attach a string to hang.

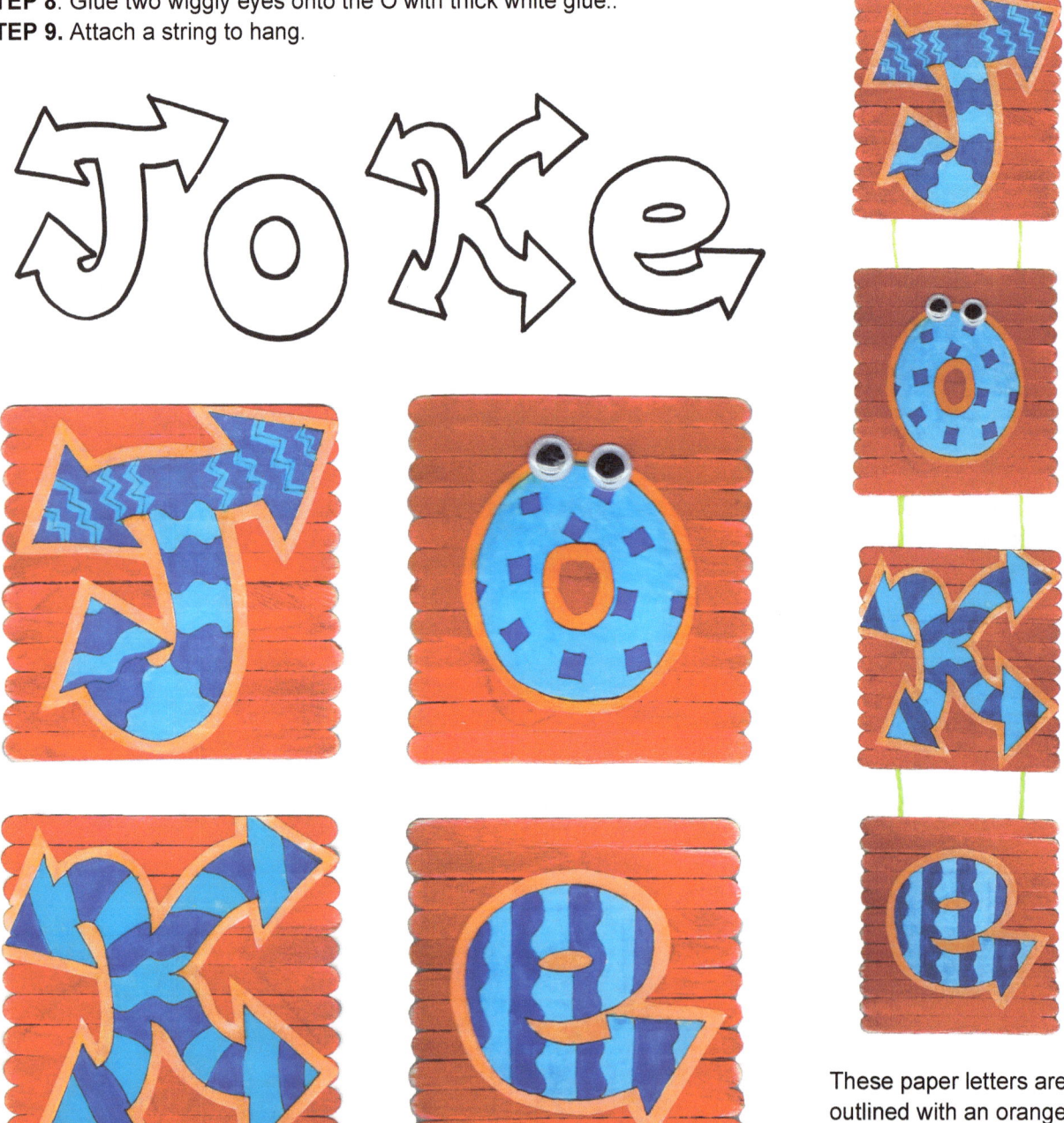

These paper letters are outlined with an orange marker and filled in with colored pencils.

You can also create freestyle letters by modifying the standard bubble letter stencils from pages 48-54. This is a helpful technique if you aren't quite ready to draw your own freestyle letters from scratch.

STEP 1. With a pencil, trace the stencils.

STEP 2. Modify the letters any way you like.

STEP 3. Draw a dark outline around the edges and erase unneeded pencil lines.

STEP 4. Make these drawings into stencils (page 10). Make paper cutouts (see page 12-13), or trace them directly onto plaques and paint (see page 11). I found some fun sports ball stickers to glue in the corners.

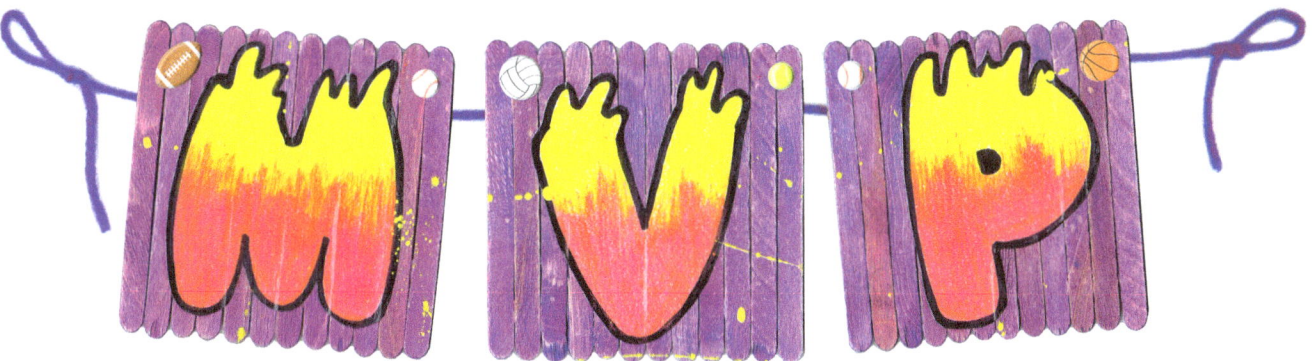

These are paper cutouts.

SO FLY

Add a little more drama to your bubble letters by making them into serif letters.

Serifs are the little flourishes on the ends of some styles of letters. Letters without these little flourishes are called sans-serif letters (sans means without). Letters with these flourishes are called serif letters.

Hang these little houses in a group in any configuration that you like. Make two, three, or four houses - any number looks great.

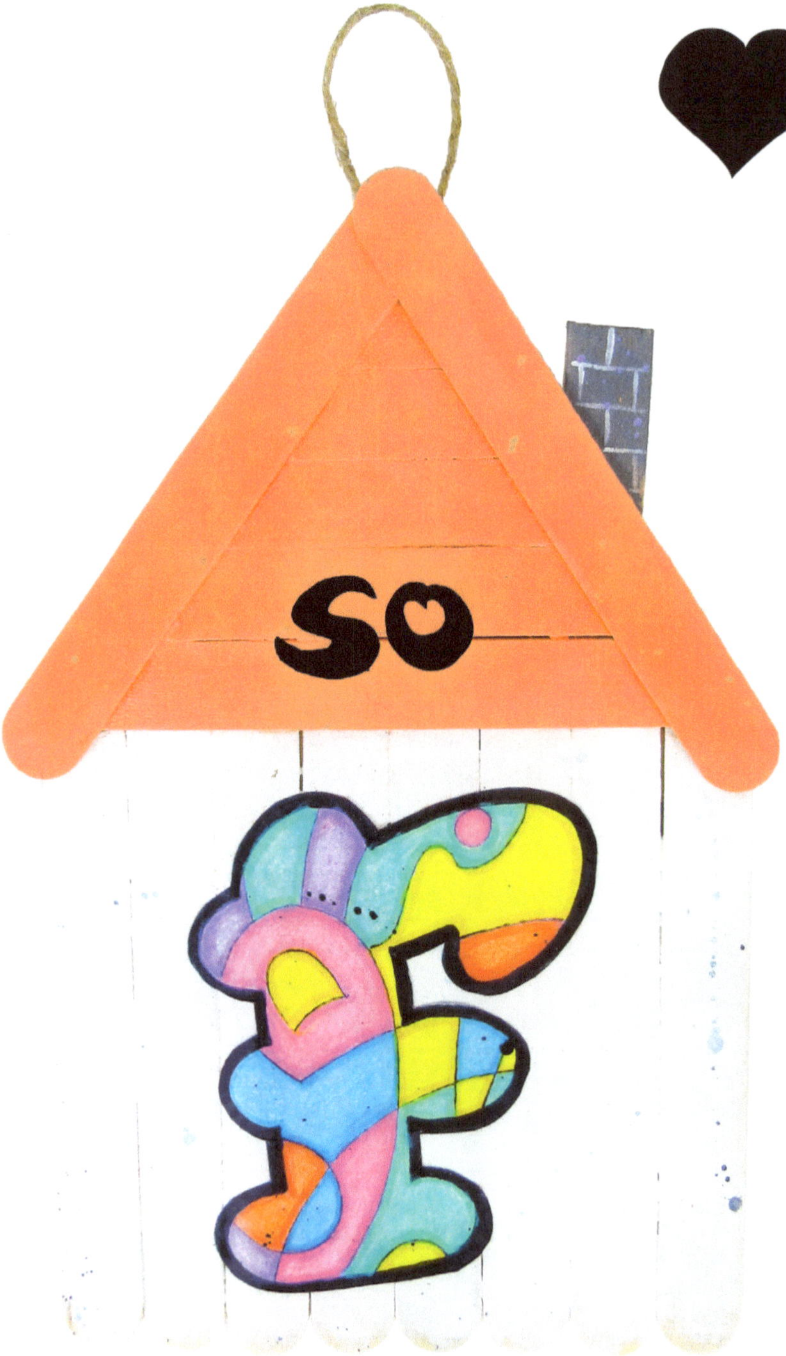

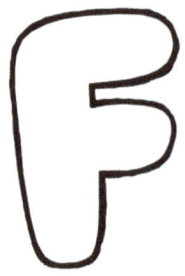

SANS SERIF
BUBBLE
LETTER

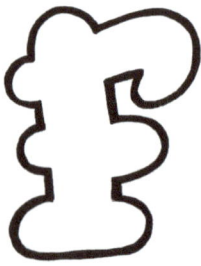

SERIF
BUBBLE
LETTER

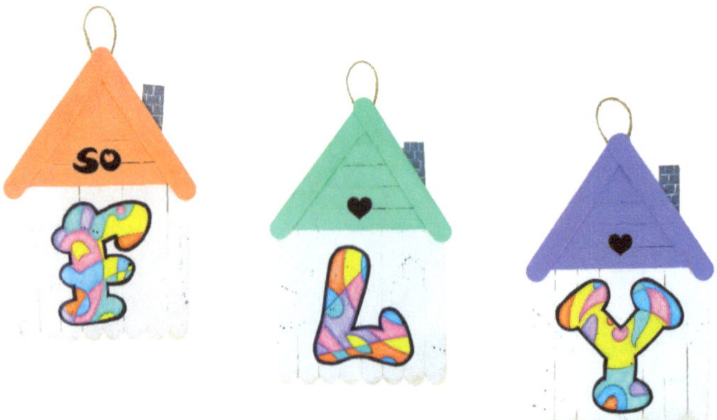

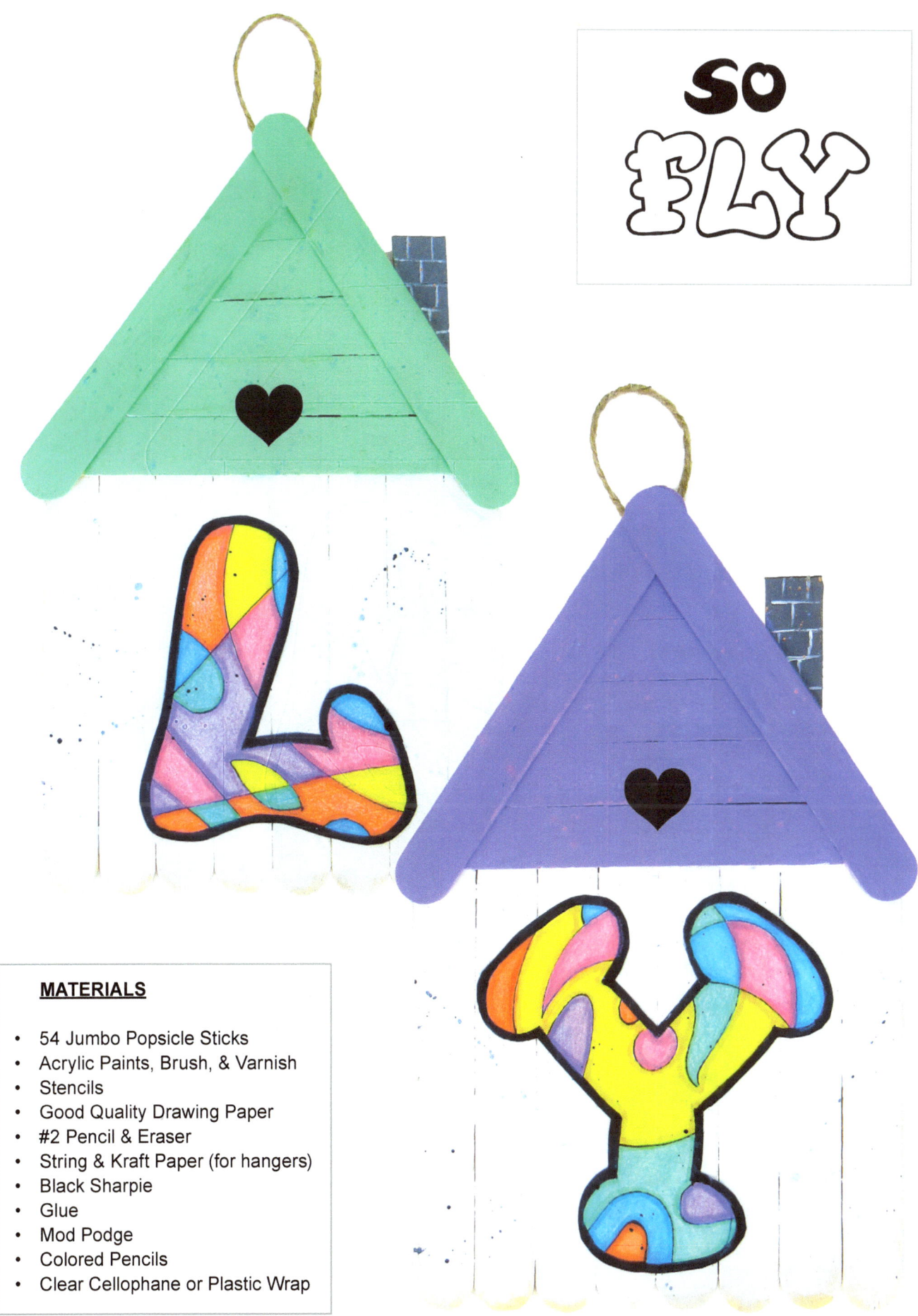

SO
FLY

MATERIALS

- 54 Jumbo Popsicle Sticks
- Acrylic Paints, Brush, & Varnish
- Stencils
- Good Quality Drawing Paper
- #2 Pencil & Eraser
- String & Kraft Paper (for hangers)
- Black Sharpie
- Glue
- Mod Podge
- Colored Pencils
- Clear Cellophane or Plastic Wrap

INSTRUCTIONS

STEP 1. Make three houses with jumbo popsicle sticks (see page 6).
STEP 2. Paint the house bodies with white paint. Paint the roofs with bright colors.
STEP 3. With a pencil, draw the letters SO on one plaque and small hearts on the other two plaques. Use the templates on page 57 as a guide.
STEP 4. Paint the SO and the hearts with black paint.
STEP 5. Splatter with tiny drops of black paint.

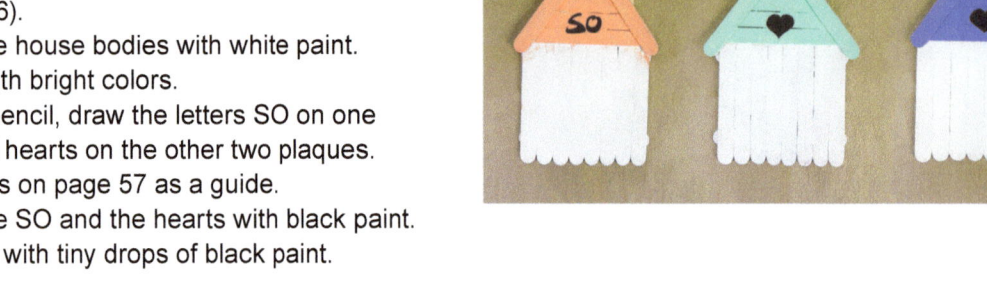

The templates for these letters are located on pages 56-57, so you can easily make the stencils to complete the project. Here is the breakdown of how I added serifs to the standard bubble letter stencils. You can use this example as a guide when you want to add serifs to any others letters. You can skip this part.

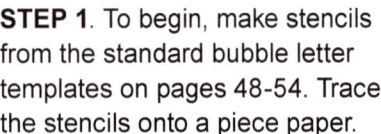

STEP 1. To begin, make stencils from the standard bubble letter templates on pages 48-54. Trace the stencils onto a piece paper.

STEP 2. Sketch small ovals on the ends of the letters to form the serifs.

STEP 3. Draw a dark outline around the outside edges of the letters and erase the pencil lines.

STEP 4. Cover the letters front and back with tape. Cut them out to make brand new stencils from your drawings (see page 10).

Complete your stencils and then move on to the next step.

1
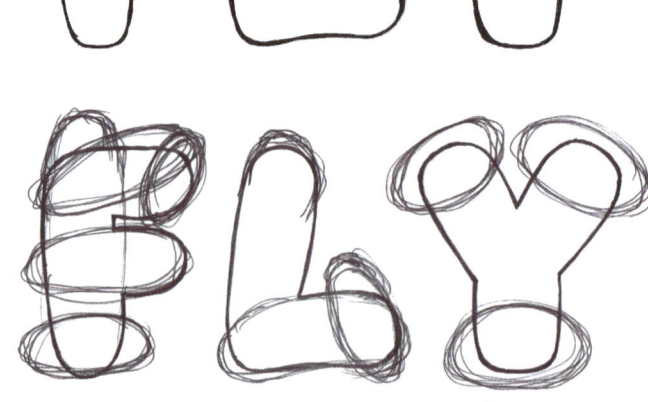

2

3
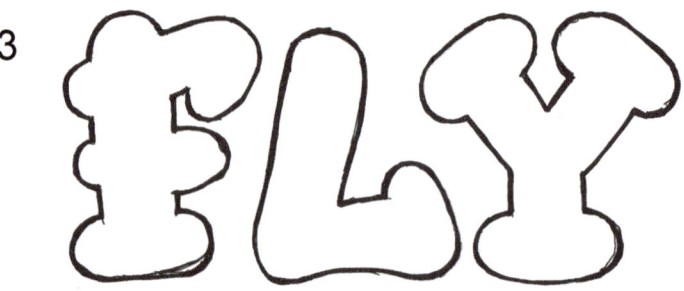

4
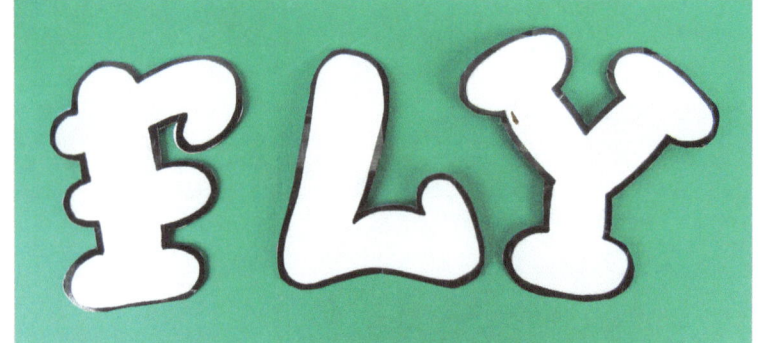

Paper Stencils

STEP 5. Draw an abstract pattern on a piece of good drawing paper with a pencil or an ultra fine-point Sharpie. Fill up the whole page.

STEP 6. Place your stencils onto the abstract pattern anywhere you like. Trace around them with a pencil. Do not overlap the edges.

STEP 7. Go over the pencil lines with dark outlines. Erase the pencil lines. Add extra shapes if needed.

STEP 8. Color in the letters with colored pencils, crayons, or magic markers.

STEP 9. Optional: Apply a coat of Mod Podge to the back of the paper.

STEP 10. Cut out each of the bubble letters.

STEP 11. Apply white glue to the backs.

STEP 12. Glue the letters onto the houses in your desired locations. Cover with clear plastic cellophane or wrap and press down firmly. Remove the plastic.

STEP 13. Brush on a light coat of varnish. Carefully varnish each color separately with a small brush so the colors don't bleed into each other. When dry, brush on a second coat over the whole piece.

STEP 14. Put hangers on the backs (see page 7).

8

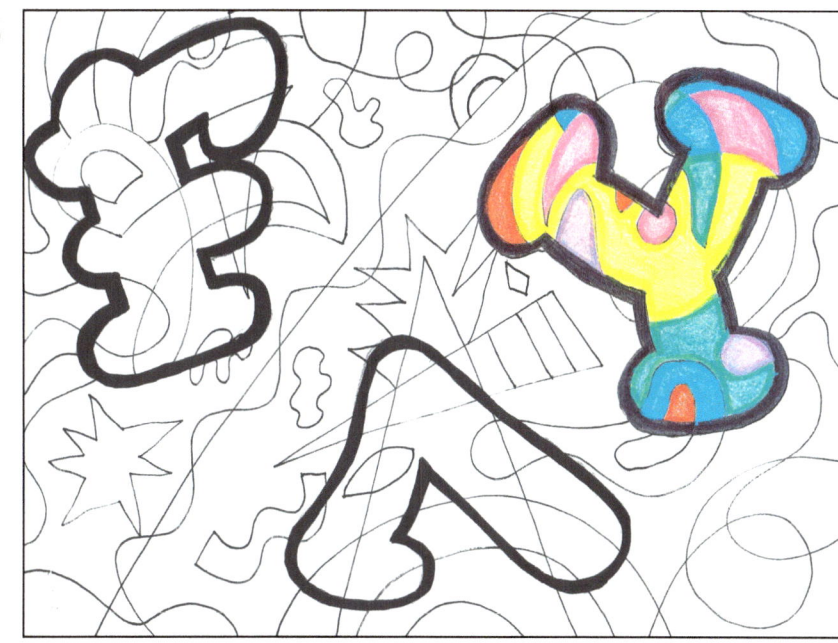

10

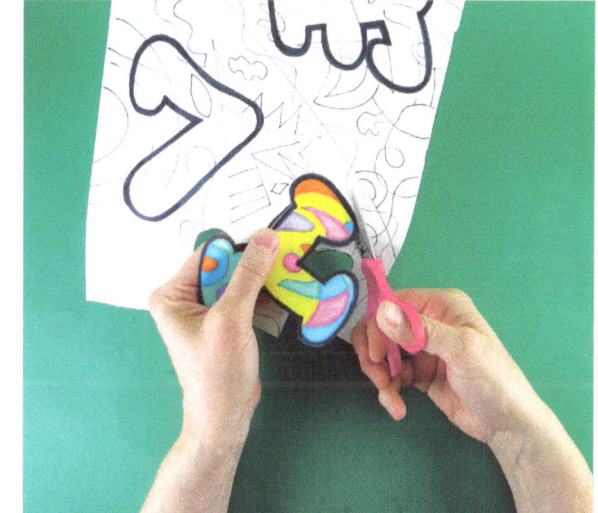

11

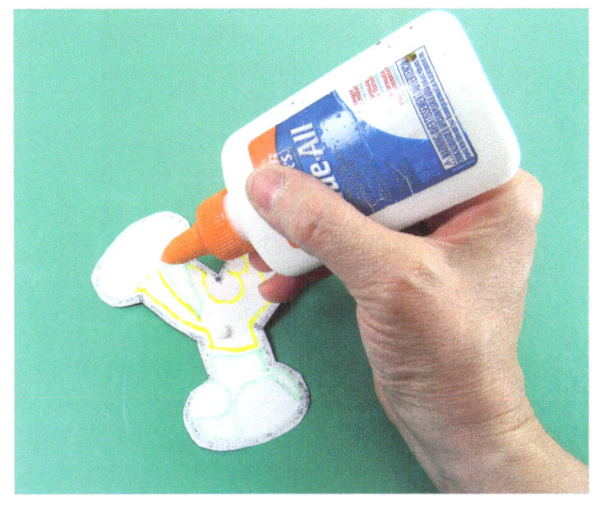

12

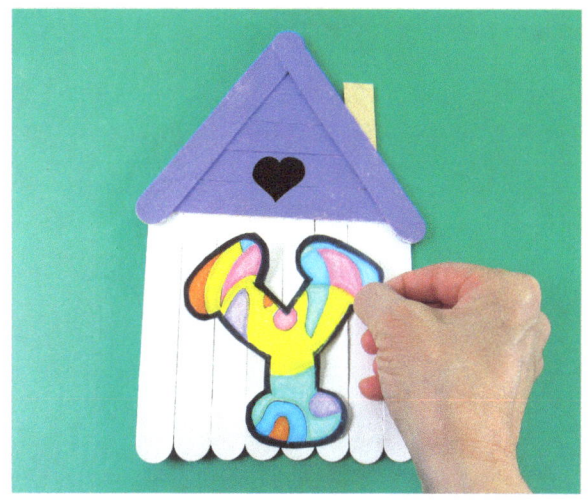

LIFE

This project is made with jumbo popsicle sticks and serif bubble letters. The letters are made from paper cutouts. You can decorate this wall hanging with any kind of small ornaments or stickers that fit into the theme of living things: dinosaurs, insects, little farm animals, butterflies, birds, fish, worms, flowers, leaves, nuts and seeds, shells, whatever you can find or dream up. Add rhinestones or sequins to the corners for a finishing touch.

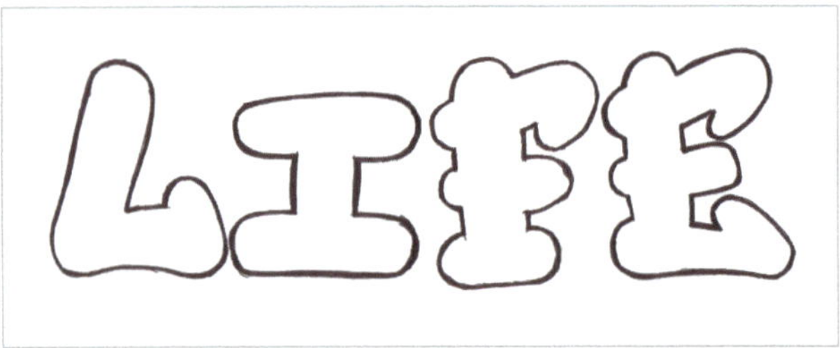

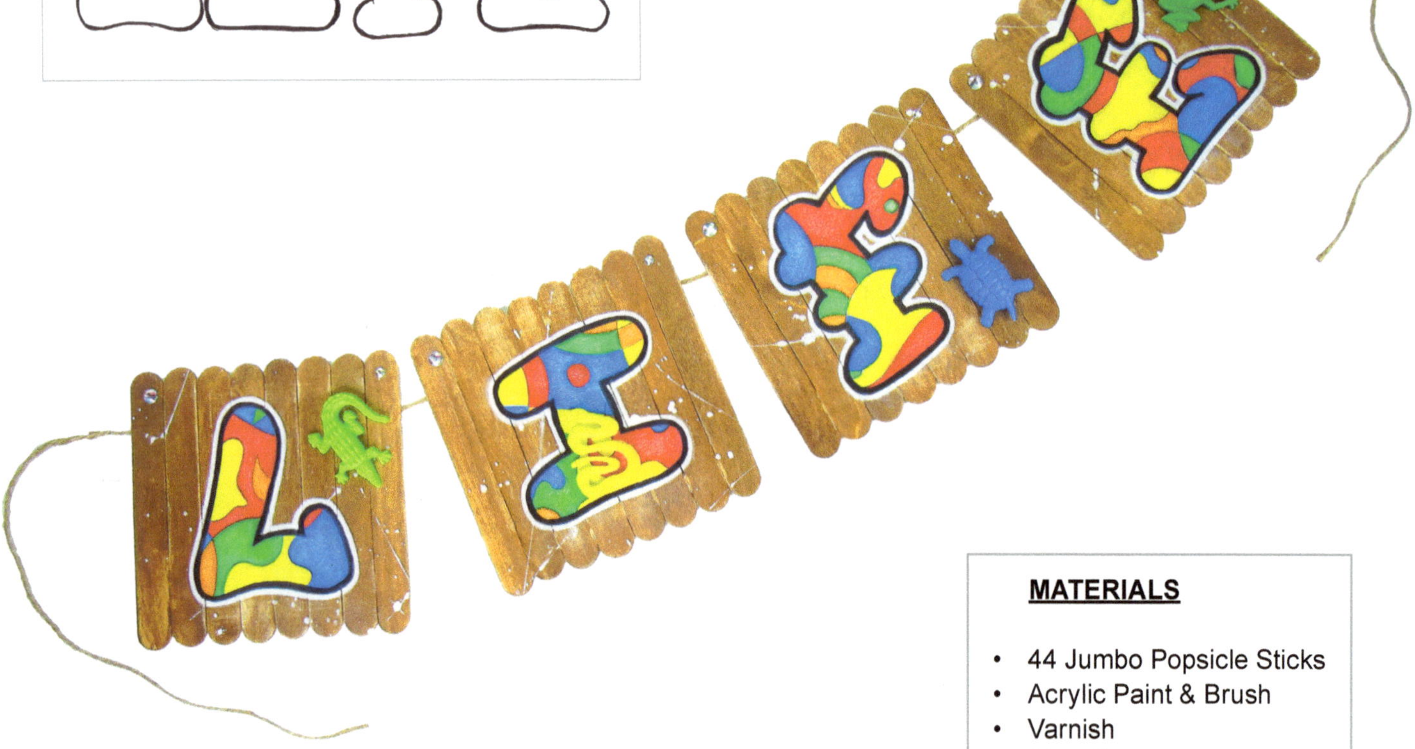

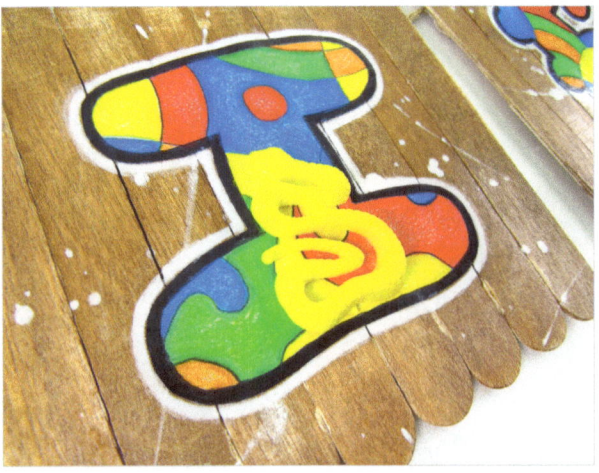

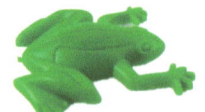

MATERIALS

- 44 Jumbo Popsicle Sticks
- Acrylic Paint & Brush
- Varnish
- Stencils
- #2 Pencil & Eraser
- Good Drawing Paper
- Twine or String
- Black Sharpie
- Glue
- Mod Podge
- Colored Pencils
- Plastic Ornaments
- Rhinestones

I found these cool little plastic reptiles at the local dollar store. I attached them with thick tacky glue. Can you see the yellow snake hiding in the abstract pattern? It's camouflaged just like a real snake would be!

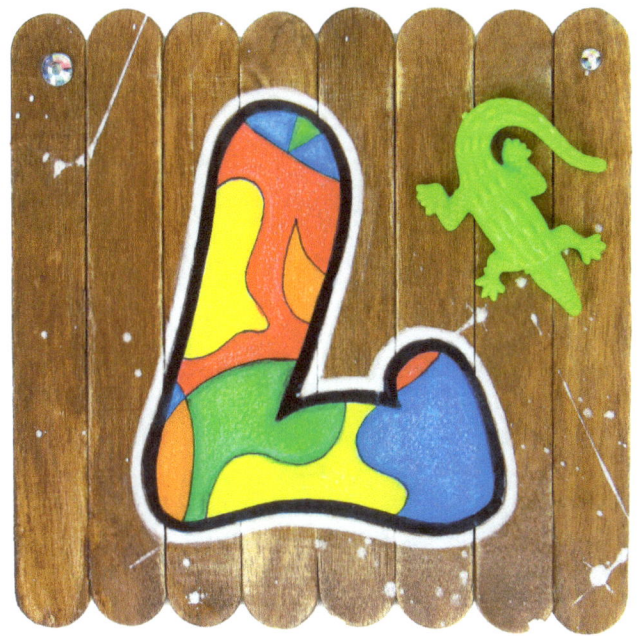

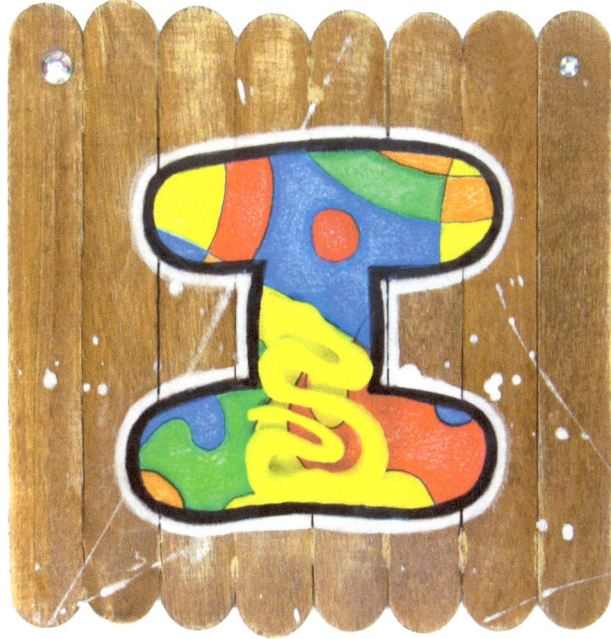

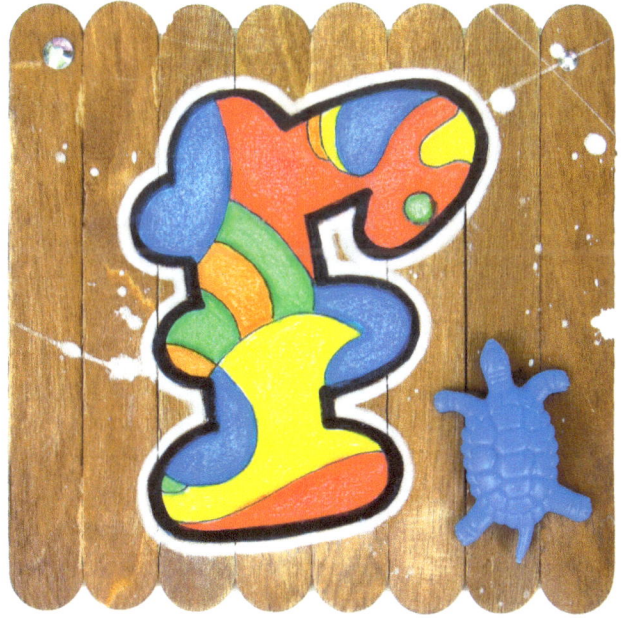

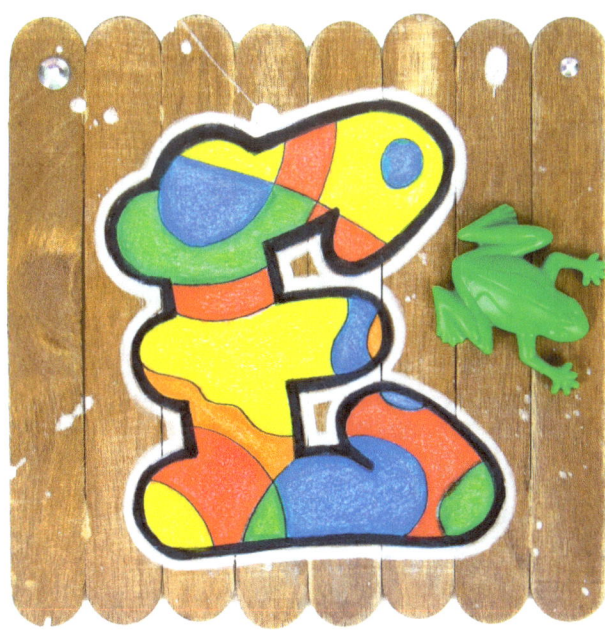

This is another project that starts with standard bubble letters which are then modified into serif letters. The finished templates are located on pages 56-57, and the breakdown is on page 46. I used colored pencils to decorate the letters in this example.

INSTRUCTIONS

STEP 1. Make four jumbo plaques (see page 4).

STEP 2. Paint with watery brown paint. Let them dry.

STEP 3. Splatter with white paint and put aside to dry.

1
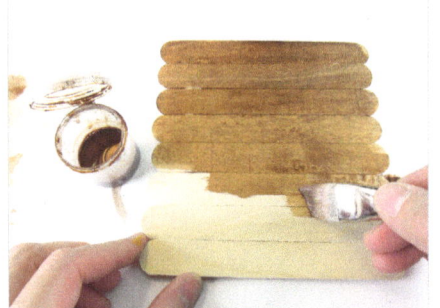

3

The finished templates for these letters are located on pages 56-57. Here is the breakdown for how to add serifs. You can use this technique to add serifs to any other letters. This project uses the same F and L from the last project, SO FLY.

STEP 1. To begin, make stencils from the standard bubble letter templates on pages 48-54. Trace them onto a piece of cheap paper with a pencil.

STEP 2. Sketch small ovals on the ends of the letters to form serifs.

STEP 3. Draw an outline around the outside edges of the letters with a dark marker. Erase the pencil lines.

STEP 4. Cover the letters front and back with tape. Cut them out to make new stencils from your finished drawings (see page 10).

When your stencils are ready, move on to the next step.

1

2

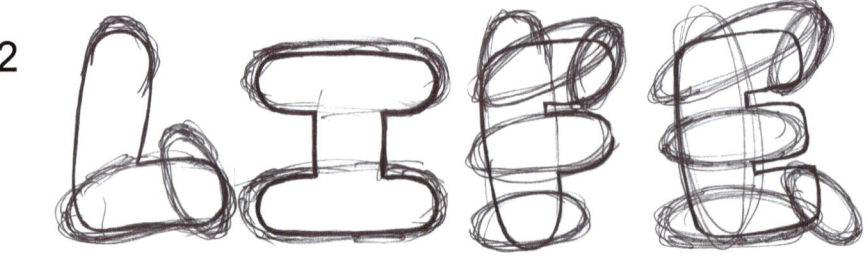

3

4

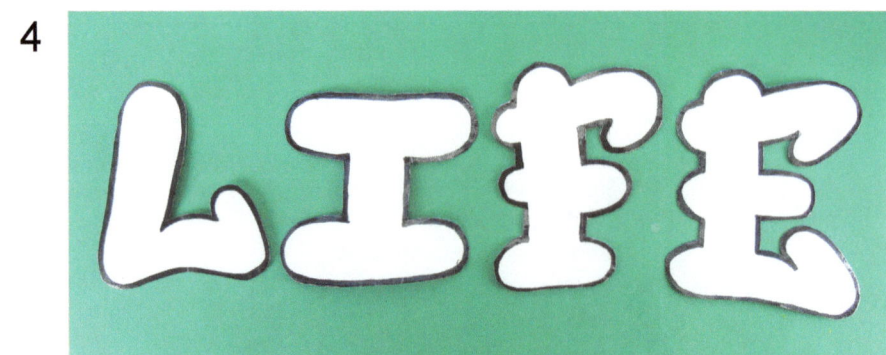

Paper Stencils

STEP 5. With a pencil or ultra-fine point marker, draw abstract patterns on two sheets of good quality drawing paper.

STEP 6. Place your serif bubble letter stencils onto the abstract patterns. Trace around them with a pencil.

STEP 7. Draw over the outlines with a black Sharpie. Erase the pencil lines.

STEP 8. Color in the letters with colored pencils, crayons, or magic markers.

STEP 9. Apply a coat of Mod Podge to the back of the letters if the paper is thin.

STEP 10. When dry, cut the letters out.

8

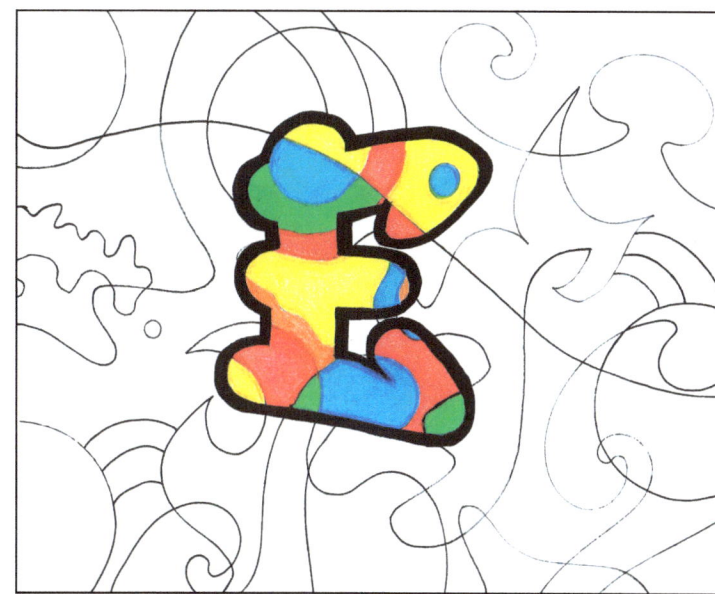

STEP 11. Glue the letters onto the plaques. Cover with plastic and press down firmly. Remove plastic.

STEP 12. Paint an outline around the letters with white paint and a tiny brush. When dry, apply a coat of varnish.

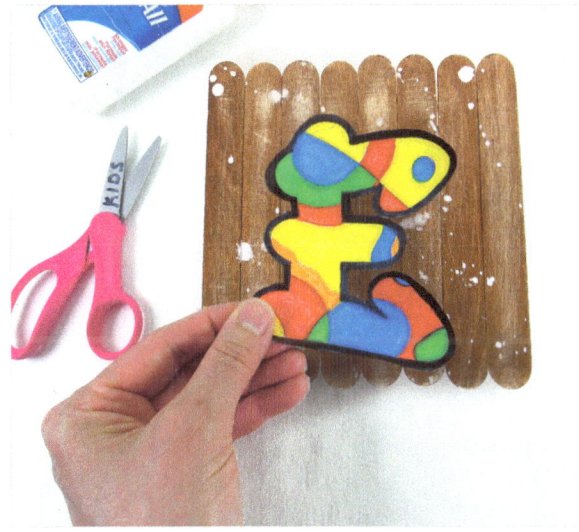

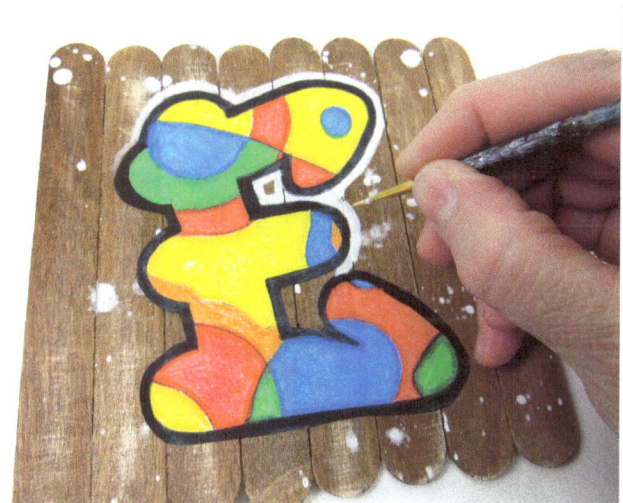

STEP 13. Attach a piece of string to the backs of the plaques (see page 9). Use a strong string, like twine.

STEP 14. Glue on plastic ornaments and rhinestones with thick tacky glue. Let the glue dry before hanging.

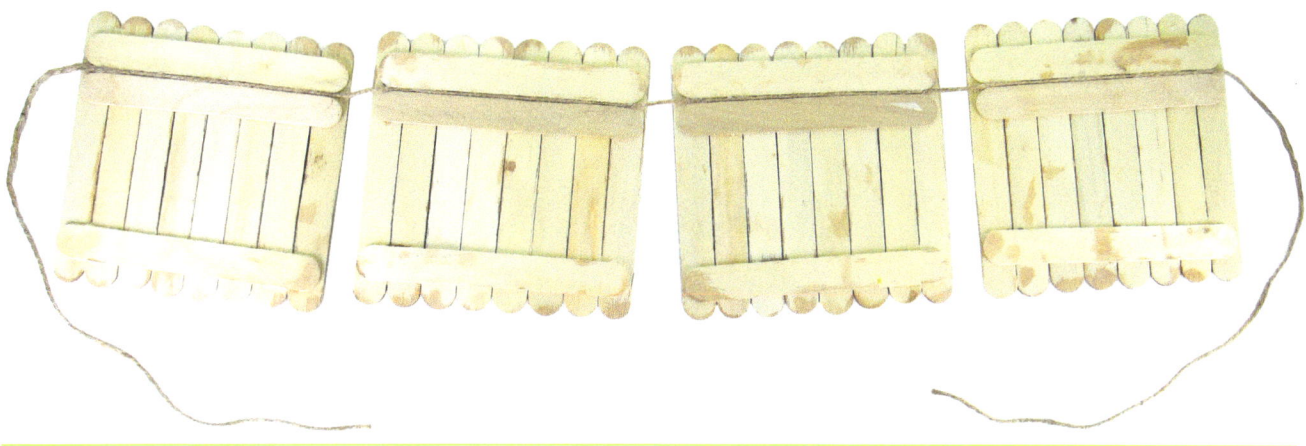

PART 3. LETTER TEMPLATES

These bubble letter templates are used to make the stencils for this book. They are sized to fit on plaques made with regular size popsicle sticks. To enlarge them to fit on plaques made from jumbo sticks you can (1) enlarge them on a copy machine, or (2) trace them and then redraw them bigger.

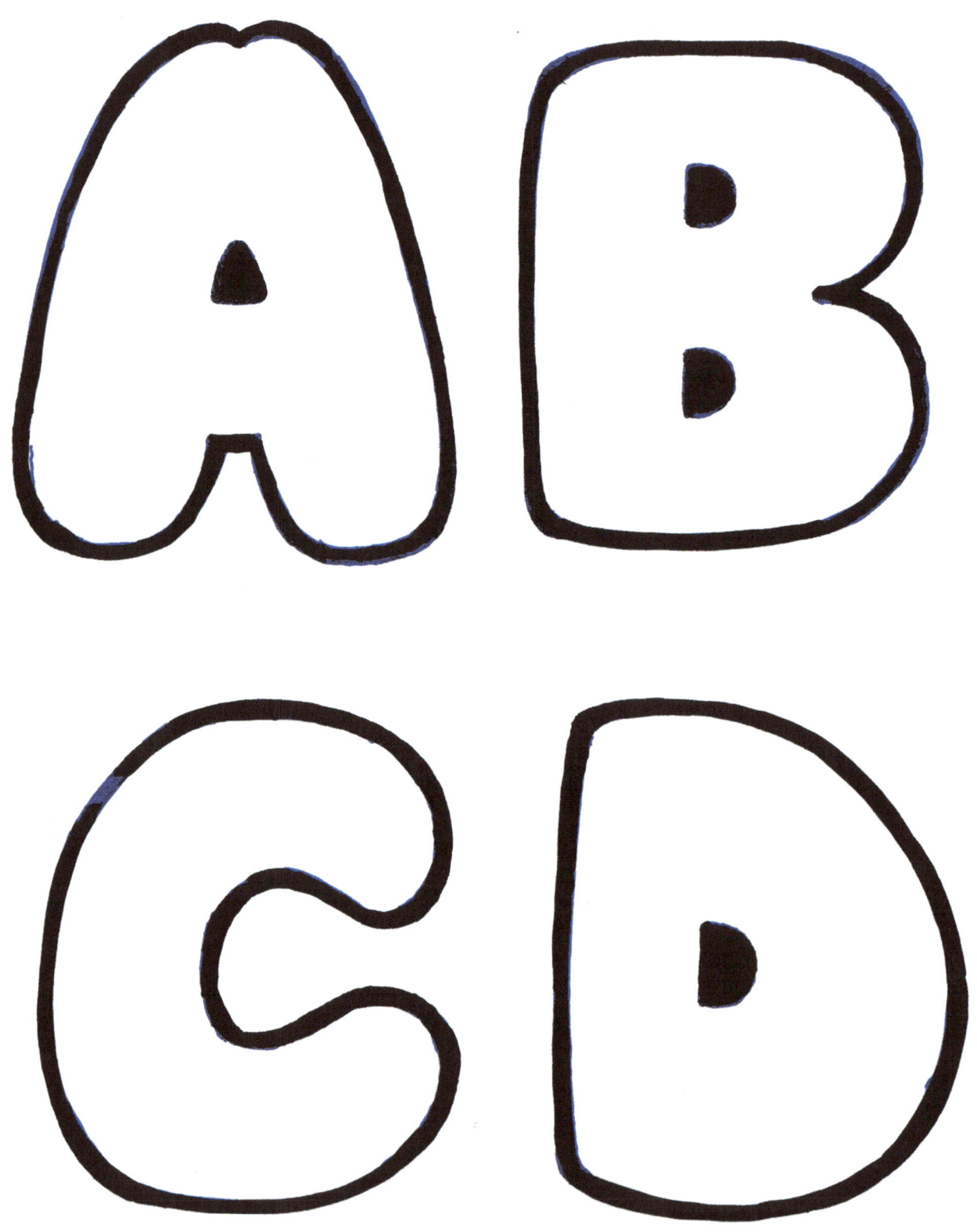

FOLLOW THESE DIRECTIONS TO MAKE STENCILS:

STEP 1. Place a piece of thin copy paper or tracing paper on top of a page and trace a letter with a pencil. Remove the paper and go over the pencil lines with a dark marking tool. Erase the pencil lines.

STEP 2. Cover the front of your letter with clear tape.

STEP 3. Cover the back of the letter with masking tape (or clear tape if that's all you have).

STEP 4. Cut the letter out. This is your finished stencil (also see page 10 for illustrated instructions).

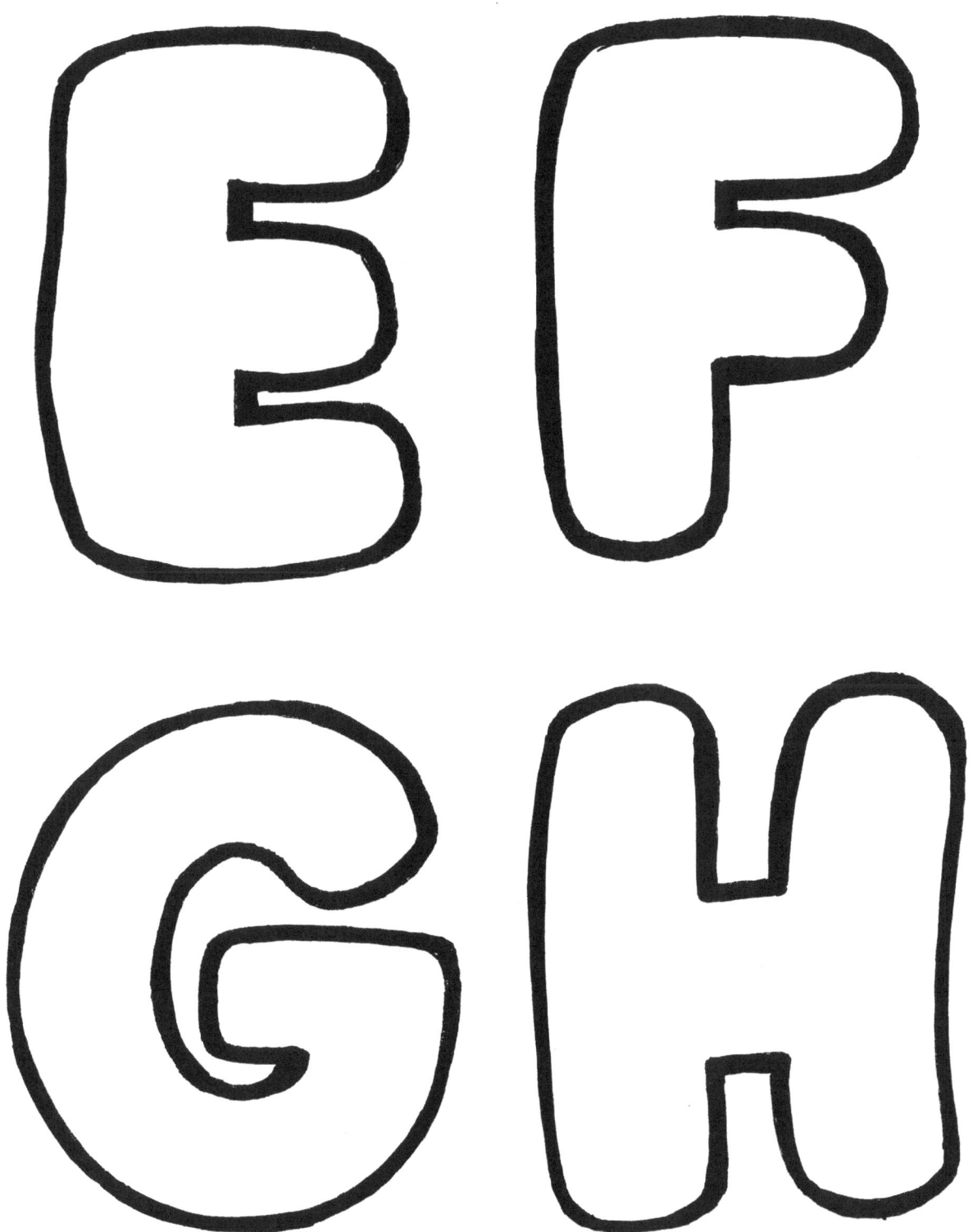

Make the stencils, trace them, and then modify the letters however you want (see page 39).

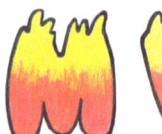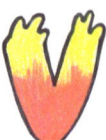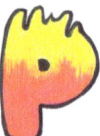

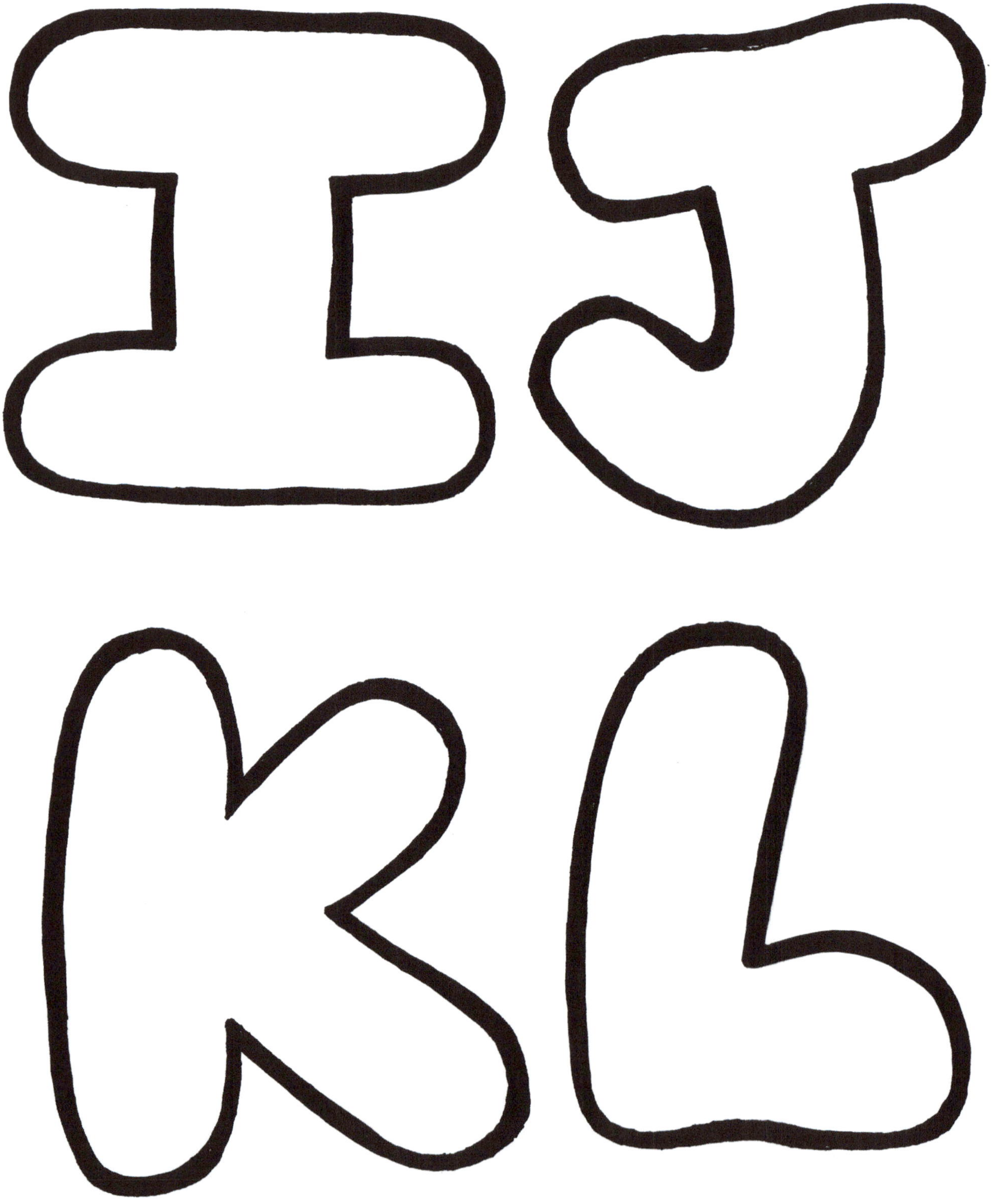

POPSICLE-STICK-GRAFFITI / NUMBER THREE

You can add a drop shadow to make the bubble letters three dimensional.

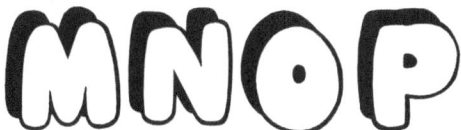

MN

OP

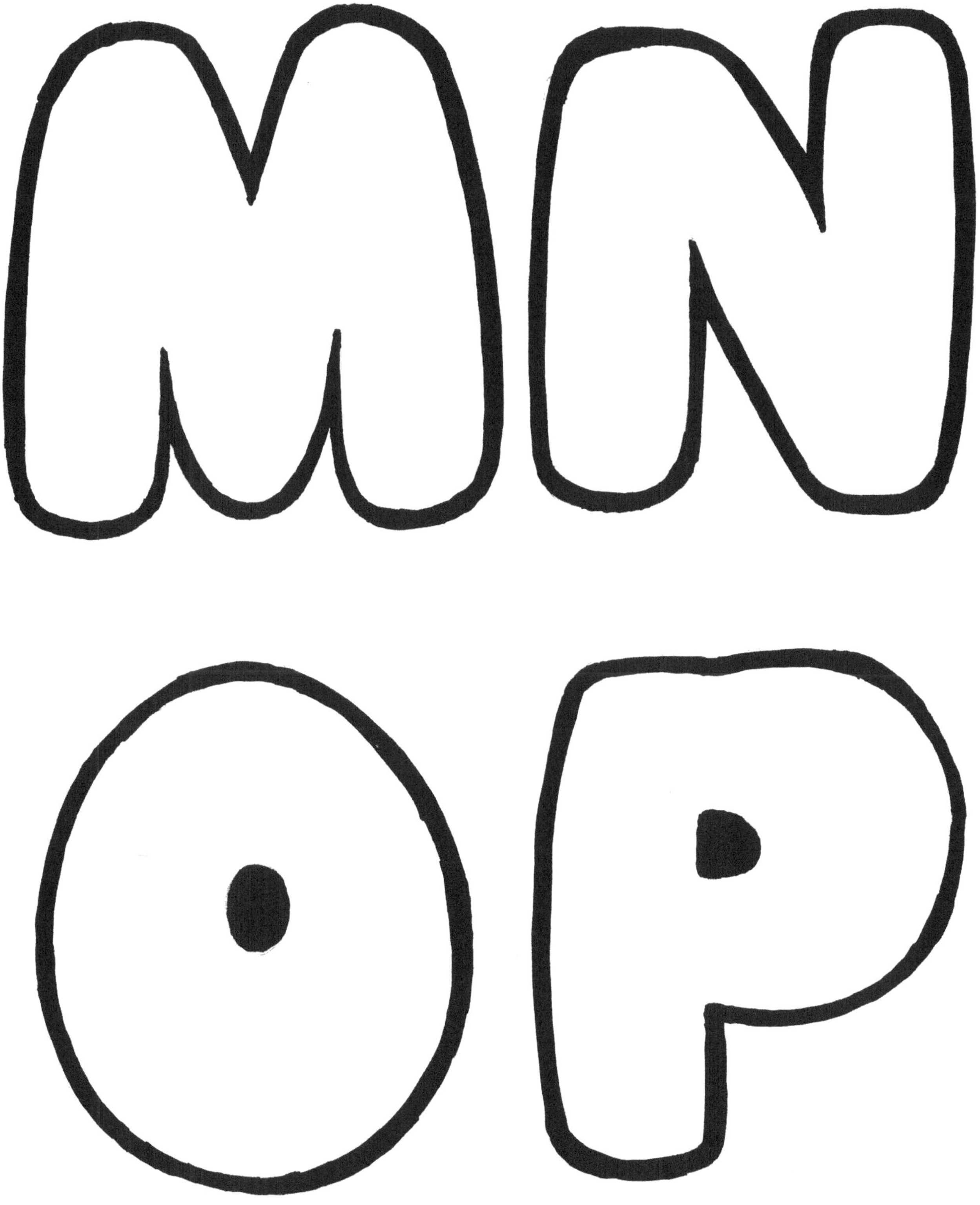

Put the drop shadow anywhere
you like - on the top, the bottom, or the side.

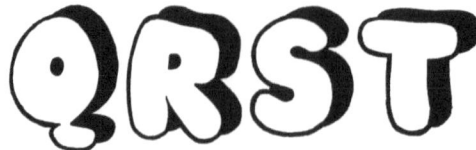

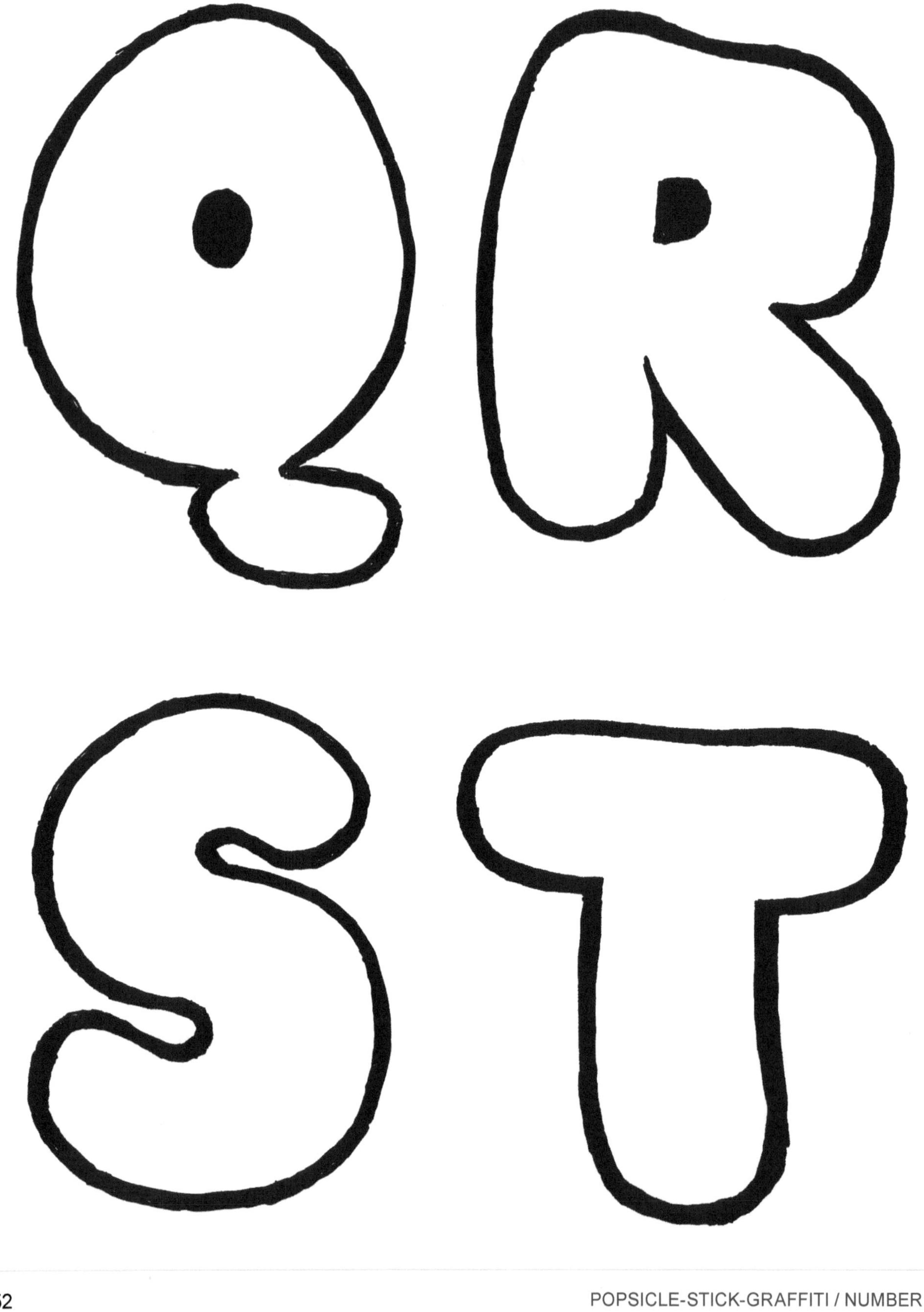

Q R

S T

POPSICLE-STICK-GRAFFITI / NUMBER THREE

U W V X

U W

V X

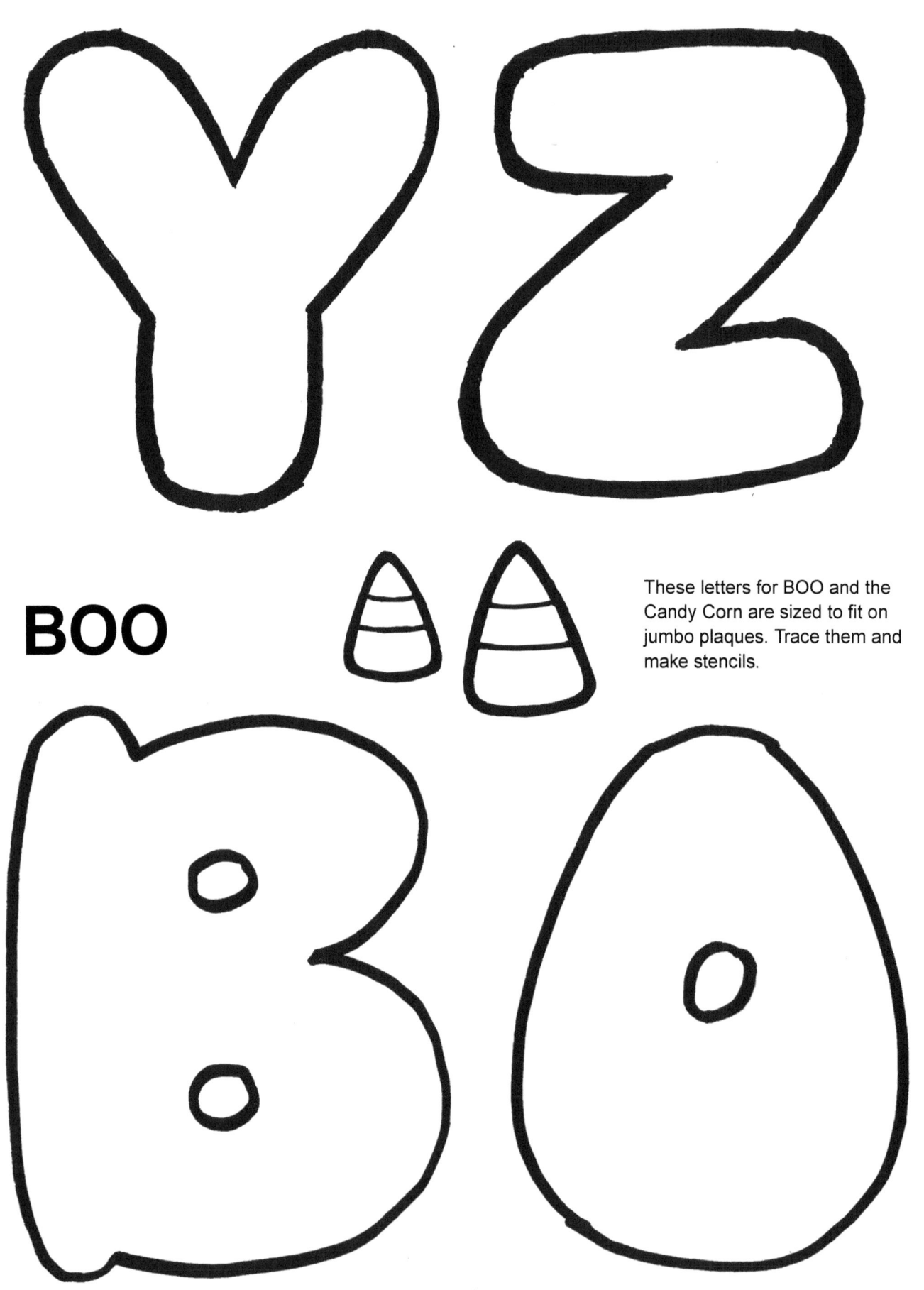

BOO

These letters for BOO and the Candy Corn are sized to fit on jumbo plaques. Trace them and make stencils.

SMILE

These SMILE letters are sized to fit on regular size plaques. The E is on the next page.

These letters for LIFE and FLY are sized to fit on jumbo plaques. Trace the templates to make stencils.

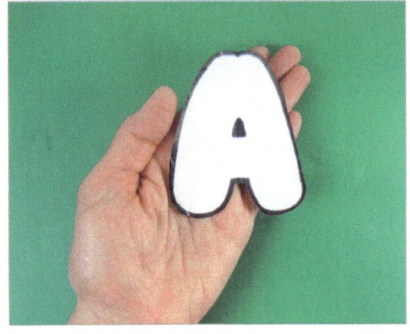

All of the stencils for the projects in this book are made from these templates on pages 48-57. The full instructions are located on page 10.

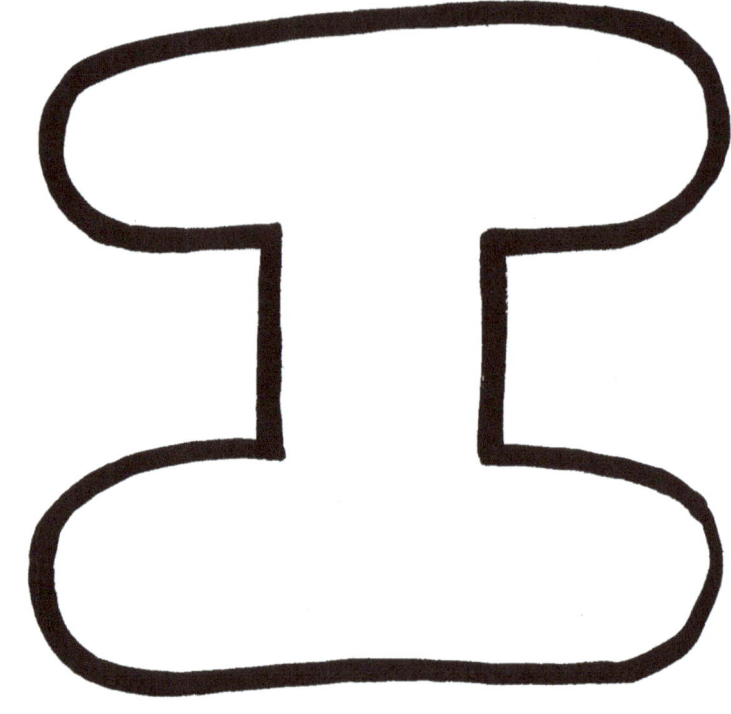

LIFE

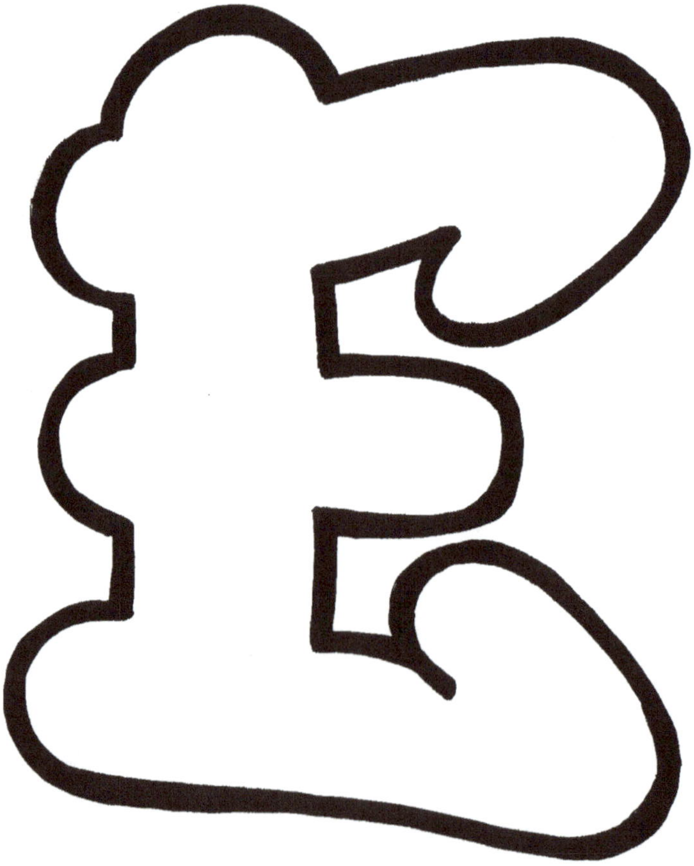

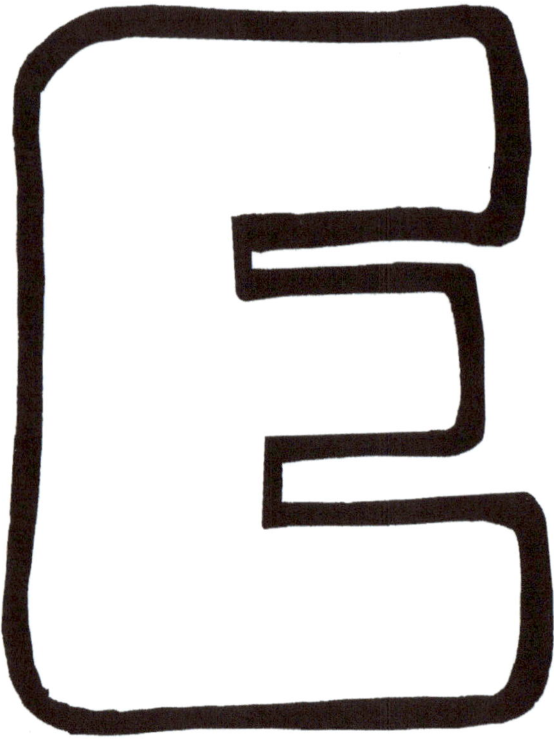

▲ This E is for
SMILE

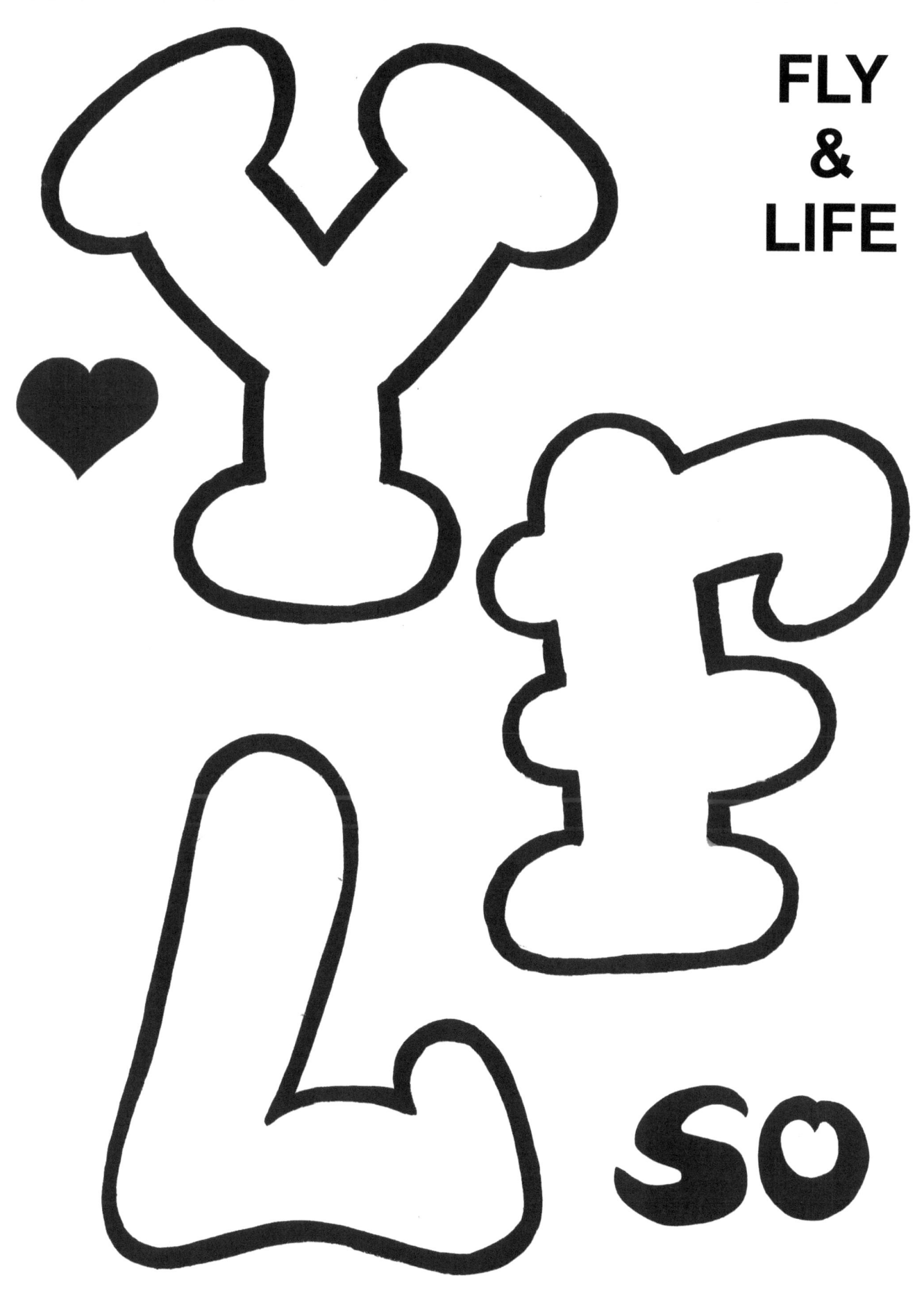

www.ingramcontent.com/pod-product-compliance
Lightning Source LLC
Chambersburg PA
CBHW050809180526
45159CB00004B/1603